living in tune

living
in
tune

21 Questions to
Activate Your Intuition
and Find Your Life Purpose

LIZ ROBERTA

HAY HOUSE
Carlsbad, California • New York City
London • Sydney • New Delhi

Published in the United Kingdom by:
Hay House UK Ltd, The Sixth Floor, Watson House,
54 Baker Street, London W1U 7BU
Tel: +44 (0)20 3927 7290; Fax: +44 (0)20 3927 7291; www.hayhouse.co.uk

Published in the United States of America by:
Hay House Inc., PO Box 5100, Carlsbad, CA 92018-5100
Tel: (1) 760 431 7695 or (800) 654 5126
Fax: (1) 760 431 6948 or (800) 650 5115; www.hayhouse.com

Published in Australia by:
Hay House Australia Pty Ltd, 18/36 Ralph St, Alexandria NSW 2015
Tel: (61) 2 9669 4299; Fax: (61) 2 9669 4144; www.hayhouse.com.au

Published in India by:
Hay House Publishers India, Muskaan Complex,
Plot No.3, B-2, Vasant Kunj, New Delhi 110 070
Tel: (91) 11 4176 1620; Fax: (91) 11 4176 1630; www.hayhouse.co.in

A catalogue record for this book is available from the British Library.

Printed in the United States of America

Tradepaper ISBN: 978-1-4019-6365-1
E-book ISBN: 978-1-78817-647-7
Audiobook ISBN: 978-1-78817-645-3

Interior illustrations: p.xi–xii Lara Skinner; p.23 Kam Bains

This product uses papers sourced from responsibly managed forests. For
more information, see www.hayhouse.com.

To Ally,

My beloved husband and soulmate,
who always believed in me.

To know you has been the greatest
joy of my life.

Light.

Light.

Light.

Love.

Love.

Love.

There is nothing above...

Only within.

Contents

Introduction

You are perfectly designed for what you are meant to do.

....

*'A soul is the most precious thing we have in
life. Without a soul, a company or a person
is nothing more than an empty shell.'*

Tadashi Yanai, owner of Uniqlo

If your mark on the world is still waiting to be made, you have
come to the right place. They say that not all who wander are
lost, but some of them are – and if that's you, I can help. I have
found my own purpose in empowering people to listen to their
intuition and tune in to their own unique spirit so that they can
align with success in all areas. Through my coaching and courses,
I've helped people to connect with themselves, attract the things
they want and create wildly successful businesses that make their
souls happy.

I created this *Living in Tune* framework of 21 questions to help my
clients who were searching for answers as to why they were put

here. At some point, we all want to know the meaning of our life. We long to feel that our arrival on Earth was for a reason, and that our being here at this exact moment in time isn't just an accident. My own opinion – and hopefully yours by the end of this book – is that you're perfectly positioned to play a role in the world like no one else can.

When you share your unique insights, talents and gifts with the world, you create a special type of impact that will reach further and feel better than anything else you do in this lifetime. The world needs you. And you can only answer that call if you're willing to side with your soul and actually *be you*. Therefore, this is a book about how to activate and access your innate intuition. When you're in tune with your intuition, you can follow your own independent path and find what is best for you – rather than what anyone else wants you to do.

Through my work at Liz Roberta Spiritual Coaching, it has become very clear to me that deep down we all know what our own calling is and we have exactly what we need to find it: our intuition. We just need to be awakened to it. The quiet calling of our soul can get lost under so many layers of 'shoulds', 'buts' and 'ifs' that we don't even recognize it anymore, but it will always stay there, itching beneath the surface of our subconscious, until we allow it to take its first breath in the physical world.

Put the distraction down when you feel the itch, and try to feel where the discomfort is coming from. The likelihood is that it's probably not because you need another glass of wine, another clothing delivery or another chocolate bar. It's because you're not accepting who you truly are and why you're really here. And I understand why it's easier to do that sometimes, because the truth can be hard to accept.

This is never more palpable than when the need for change threatens to loom over the life you've spent years building, like a tsunami of realizations that could wash away all of your old reasoning. Without deciding to jump on board with our intuition, catch the wave and ride with it, it'll end up being a wipeout, with limbs flailing in all directions and surfboard astray – as it was for me. But I believe it was that way for me so that I could warn people, and so that I'd be able to help you ride through your life with more ease and flow. I think this because, ultimately, I believe that we can choose to see how life is always working for us rather than against us.

There are lessons hidden everywhere – in every heartbreak, failure, loss and disappointment. There is always an opportunity to rise and ascend to the next level from something that didn't work before. If your truth is that you're trusting yourself and your own inner wisdom to know what's best for you, then you can feel safe in the knowledge that you're always being guided to wherever you're meant to be. Even when you find yourself in the middle of a difficult lesson, time will often reveal how you're being gifted an opportunity for expansion and growth. You can make your experiences a soundboard to fine-tune you for success.

My out of tune days

I wish I'd been born understanding this, but the truth is that my life's journey was routed for me to figure it out the hard way. If I'd never been schooled in listening to my own intuition, then I'd never be able to help guide people back to theirs. I definitely didn't always know that there was this thing called 'intuition' and that I should be listening to it, but I've been spiritual ever since I was a small, strange child. I'd cut out spells from *Mizz* magazine and stuff them into the pockets of a red plastic folding wallet I had, which grew larger and larger each week until it eventually formed the CV of a part-time witch. As well as doing hocus pocus to make a boy in my Year 6 class like me, I'd spend my £5-a-week pocket money on incense, essential oils and the coloured candles I needed to perform manifestation rituals in my bedroom. Even then, I was a little manifestor and was guided by a deep belief that I could create anything I wanted.

At 14, a friend connected me with Tarot cards for the first time, but for the next decade my spirituality got pushed to the side in favour of drinking, partying, studying for exams and following the 'normal' way. This version of 'normal' I was trying to achieve was an idea of reality that had been subtly pressed upon me by society and the people around me, so I valued that model of reality way above my own intuition and what actually felt good for me.

Once I was able to see some light again, after the black hole that was my teenage years, it was already too late. I'd taken actions to create outcomes that literally couldn't have been less aligned with who I am and what I enjoy doing. The truth is: if we're not in alignment then we're out of alignment. We can make excuses and try to cover it up as much as we like, hiding behind the practicalities and reasons why we can't make changes, but the feeling will persist until we do something about it.

When I look back at my out of tune days, I don't know whether to laugh or cry first. I worked so hard to get into a top university, thinking that my exam grades would be my golden ticket to freedom. Unfortunately, I was wrong and I spent the next three years of my life dragging myself through an economics degree that made me miserable. 'I'll get us out of this!' yelled my ego, with such conviction that it jolted me into action yet again, this time to hustle my way onto a graduate scheme at the world's leading investment bank. 'This will be different, I'm sure of it!'

Why I thought it was a good idea to take a job in something I already knew I hated, I don't know, but at that point in my early 20s I was fully invested in singing from someone else's hymn sheet. There was nothing in tune, and if anything, I was so used to the sound of bum notes and dodgy chords from the different parts of my life clashing together that it practically lulled me to sleep at night. My soul was right and I was wrong. *Who knew that a well-paid job with good benefits really isn't the answer to everything after all?*

My soul stung and my ego was bruised. On completion of the two-year graduate scheme, I caught the last bus (which I'd affectionately named the prison bus) out of there with my tail between my legs and vowed to do something more exciting with my life – something glamorous, wild and full of vivid colour rather than the rainbow of greys and blacks that painted the entire banking world. The fun of fashion was calling me and I answered, tottering towards it as fast as I could in my prized pair of Louboutins I'd bought with my first 'proper' pay cheque. There was promise here, between the pages of *Vogue*, and the creative freedom to express myself with reckless abandon; not only was brilliance and boldness accepted here, it was encouraged.

After getting a scholarship onto a master's degree, which was a serene interlude between my careers in the worlds of finance and fashion, I followed the freebies. That's right: the free shoes, handbags and press goodie bags that I knew would fulfil some kind of *The Devil Wears Prada* dream for me. Yes, there were press days out of the office, catwalk shows and days in London shopping at Harrods ('do I really get paid for this?'); but no, I was still not in tune. The office was still windowless, and sunlight was a rare commodity; the days were long and now included regular trips into work at weekends, for less money; but worst of all, there was still a gaping hole where a sense of purpose was missing.

My saving grace was that in the one month I had free between finishing my master's and starting my new career in fashion, I had the time and mental space to dive deep into the things I'd always been naturally guided towards. Without thinking, I'd find myself clicking through videos on YouTube about energy, mindset and manifestation. With every third-eye-opening meditation I listened to, and each uplifting talk I watched on how to free my mind of limitations, I felt more of my intuition awakening. By trial and error I eventually found out what I'm really here for, and now I get to enjoy the satisfaction of knowing this every single day. I can see now that life is perfectly orchestrated for us to get the best out of it we possibly can, so when it seems as though the structures that we've made are breaking down, or that the life we used to love no longer fits us, we can be sure that it's because we're on the edge of a beautiful new beginning.

Your gifts are unique

I developed the *Living in Tune* framework by figuring out what I could create that would help people to tune in to their soul and connect with themselves. The gift you have to offer has a unique place in the world, and by following this process, it'll become a lot clearer what you're really here for and what your soul most wants you to do. When you follow your feelings and trust that your inner intuition is more important than external influences from anyone else, you can find fulfilment in a way that you've never found it before. Everything will slot into place and you will be able to hold yourself high as the ultimate knower and sovereign source of your own guidance.

Everyone's intuition is different: some people have clear psychic sight, while others simply have clear insights. These insights often come through as an unexplained deep knowing or as a physical feeling. We're all familiar with the term 'gut feeling', and through all the work I've done with clients, I've found this to be the most common way people access their intuition – they can feel when something is a good or bad idea. As everyone can tap into their intuition in many different ways, throughout this book I've included various techniques for you to try, so you can see what works best for you. Whether it's through your eyes, ears, mind, gut or external signs, there are so many ways to guide yourself towards an easier life of fun and flow.

However you decide to use what your intuition tells you, you'll find it hard to ignore once you know the answer. There's no feeling like doing something that's aligned with your unique life purpose – it feels so easy that it actually fills you up with energy, rather than draining you because you're always pushing against resistance from your soul. Problems are less daunting to face once you know why you're committed to facing them, and the solutions arrive more effortlessly than when you're trying to solve something that was never right for you in the first place. Flowing is your natural state, so it's simply a case of removing any obstacles limiting the life force that flows through you.

Your purpose is simply the place where your soul feels at home because it's completely in tune with the life that you're living. And even though I've described my own career journey, it's important to remember that your sense of purpose won't necessarily be found in a job or career. For some people this will be the case, and they'll be lucky enough to feel the benefits of finding fulfilment, making an impact and enjoying endless satisfaction while also earning an income at the same time. But this definitely isn't true for everyone, and that's okay too – your purpose isn't necessarily your career. Your sense of purpose can come from a whole range of things: from having your children and being a great parent; from writing a book that you put together each morning before you head off to work; or from connecting people together.

How to know if you're out of tune

Even if you're completely at a loss as to what your sense of purpose is at the moment, your intuition is still guiding you there because you'll be aware of all the things that are definitely *not* it. The polarity of this Universe we live in means that we often understand what something *is* through experiencing what it *is not*, so you'll already be far along your journey if you're able to rule out all the things that are out of tune for you. There are some very clear signs that you might notice in yourself – or in the people closest to you if they're far along a journey of uncovering everything that's out of tune for them. If you can see someone struggling because they're out of tune with their intuition, then please be sure to gift this book to them.

Being out of tune can have these symptoms:

✦ You're struggling to sleep well and having vivid dreams or nightmares; this means that throughout the day you're fighting a constant urge to rest, nap and sleep.

✦ You may have physical signs of tension, such as headaches, nausea, feeling faint and/or lethargic; possibly accompanied by general aches, pains and health complaints.

✦ Something feels 'off' but you can't quite put your finger on exactly what it is.

✦ General confusion about where you're going makes it hard for you to decide your next step forwards.

✦ You might feel detached, disorganized and a bit 'all over the place'; this happens when your physical and inner self are living different versions of your reality.

✦ You may experience loneliness from struggling to connect with other people, because you're not fully connected with yourself.

✦ You often feel lethargic and unmotivated because you're not doing what you really want to do.

✦ You might notice yourself feeling bitter about other people's happiness and jealous of their success, when you know that you're a loving person deep down.

✦ You're anxious and unsure about the future because you don't know what would make you feel better or where to go next. As a result, you're struggling to appreciate and have gratitude for where you are right now.

Tuning back in to your intuition

Now for the good news! When you're following your intuition and channelling its inspiration through your actions, it has the power to completely change your life. Things will start to make sense and you can edit your reality based on what feels good for you and what doesn't. You'll notice how relationships enter or leave your life at exactly the right time, and your self-love will soar as you realize all of the ways you're already brilliant. You'll be rooted in your own power, which is a place where you'll become more immune to criticism from the shadow part of your own mind and from other people. It's a lot harder to be a victim of self-doubt when you – in your heart – have no doubt about who you are, why you're here and what you're meant to be doing.

Following your intuitive guidance is also the secret to success in all its forms, because more intuitively led action creates more abundance, especially if you have your own business. Getting in tune with what you love allows more energy to enter and flow through you into the things you do. This magical life force that you breathe into your projects, passions and paid work will channel through to the lives it's meant to touch. When you're aligned, not only can you manifest more easily, but you can create the huge impact that you're here to make. Whatever legacy you're meant to leave the world with is finally possible once you know how to follow your own guidance and take the first step.

The most amazing result I've seen from asking my clients these questions is that, once they know they can trust themselves and how they feel, they gain confidence. By answering these questions to get acquainted with the different facets of yourself – your personality, your journey, your talents, what feels like paradise – you'll see what your unique life journey has been guiding you towards. As with everything I teach about intuition online and with my clients, it's not about someone telling you what you 'should' be doing; it's about you feeling what's true and right for *you*, because only you know the answers for your own life.

How to use this book

For the remainder of this book, I'll be guiding you through a journey of 21 questions that relate to 21 words beginning with the letter P – like the word 'Purpose'. The things that make us feel most joyful are important signposts for us to follow, so each of these 21 questions will help you to distinguish when your intuition is saying a great big 'yes' or hard 'no' to something. By tuning in to how you're feeling and recognizing the difference, you'll be able to align yourself with an everyday life filled with more of what you love and less of what you don't. There are big P-shaped clues hiding within our feelings, desires and talents because we're perfectly designed for what we're meant to do.

This book is a practical guide to help you awaken your intuition and connect with a more purposeful life, so it's filled with 'Intuition in action' exercises. These are a mix of actionable techniques, journalling activities and opportunities for self-discovery and reflection. If you do all of these exercises, you'll find that you get much more used to actually putting your intuition into practice, because when you just read about something as words, you don't necessarily integrate the teachings as much as when you learn them through your own experience.

There are also some client case studies, when I've worked with people whose experiences perfectly epitomize the lesson within a certain chapter. Sharing their stories shows you that it's possible to transform and up-level your life by committing to your intuition alone. As well as the main question, which is the focus of each chapter, there are also three 'Go deeper' journalling questions at the end. After you've read every chapter, use a journal to write down each question one at a time, before sitting with it and seeing which answer wants to come out.

Feel into the words and empty your mind as much as possible. Let answering these questions be an opportunity to experience what it's like when your intuition speaks to you. Try not to rush them, because you really want to get to the root of what your answers are instead of hurrying through them (which can be your ego's way of avoiding a truth that you really need to know). If there's a question that you get particularly stuck on and don't feel you can answer, just leave it and come back to it, because the answer might pop into your head when you're not expecting it and not thinking about anything (that's often the way intuition works). Answering all of the questions in this book will be endlessly revealing about who you are at a soul level and what you really want from life. Then, if you can start making choices based on what you've learned about yourself, you'll find that your life fits you so much better.

On my website – www.LizRoberta.com/LivingInTune – you can access a whole portal of free goodies to help you with this process. You'll have access to a free 'Tune Out & Tune In' meditation that will help you to tune out the noise and connect with your intuition. You will also get a free printable workbook with all of these questions in it, so you can journal through all of your answers to the *Living in Tune* framework.

Through this journey that we're about to take together, I intend for you to find every part of yourself that has been forgotten, lost or set aside. Each part of you is valuable and each part of you is here for a purpose. Everything that you have gone through has been preparing you for your greatest destiny and, by following the clues in how you feel, what you see and where you think there could still be improvement, you can finally feel at home in the life you truly deserve.

Your feelings are always guiding you and no one knows what path will fit you better than you, because you're the only one who is going to be walking it. It's not always the easiest option to go your own way – which is why most people aren't doing it – but it's the only life that's going to fit you perfectly. If you feel that everything has been wrong up until this point, you can choose to change it now, because it's never too late to turn your life around. It's time to set your intuition free so that you can be who you were always meant to be. Tune out the noise and tune in to what feels true and right for you. The world is waiting for you to make your mark.

Power

Question 1: When does the greatest version of you come out?

. . . .

'You have to find that place that brings out the human in you. The soul in you. The love in you.'

R.M. Drake

Your intuition is your greatest source of power. When you know who you really are and what direction you really want to go in, a certain type of unstoppable certainty roots you deep into the ground and stops you being swayed by outside forces. When you catch a glimpse of yourself shining because something lights you up from the inside, that's a signal that you're standing in your power, like a lighthouse that stands firm whatever the storm and shines night and day, regardless of what's going on around it. If something sways you out of your power, you'll know by how quickly the storm takes over and plunges you back into the darkness.

The first step of awakening your intuition so that you can live a more in tune life is to find when the most authentic side of you comes out, so you can identify with that part of you more often. It's through activating your intuition that you awaken the biggest, best and most powerful version of you. Once you see when you're most powerful, it will make it harder for you to stay in the things that keep you stuck, stagnant and living a life that makes you feel out of tune.

What is your definition of power?

Maybe you wouldn't equate intuition with power, but after spending years in spirituality, working with very gifted clients who have created huge success based on their intuitive guidance, I know that the strongest power is often the most secretive of all – the one that no one likes to discuss and the type that never makes news headlines. Before we go into this chapter, I want first to address any feelings of resistance that might come up around this particular P-word. Yes, for many years, power has been hegemonized and used to control and conquer, but the power that comes from being aligned with our soul is sensitive to the greater good. It's by being the best person we can be that we contribute the most to the world – which is why we need to realize when the best version of us reveals itself, because it's intricately tied to how we can add the most to the whole through our own unique sense of purpose.

Imagine how different the news would be if the world was led by intuition rather than ego? It's the same for our personal life. The decisions that we make seeking power from a place of ego are usually driven by insecurity or a need for external validation, leading to dubious results and disastrous outcomes. However, when we're guiding ourselves from the innate power of our intuition, it leads to outcomes that make us feel good, in tune and empowered in a completely new way.

I always say that spirituality can be your superpower and your success secret, because it's through your spirituality that you gain access to the infinite: knowledge, wisdom and open opportunities. People in power operating from ego are restricted to the extent of only what they can reach within the limited human mind. Your personal power is something unique to you and to find out what it is and how it relates to your purpose, you need to notice when you start to see the version of yourself that you most like and respect.

Your secret source of power

Another way your intuition gives you power is by creating a direct, unhindered channel to your soul source of life force energy. Have you noticed how, when you're doing something that you don't want to do, you have to push and force yourself (all while moaning and giving yourself frown lines)? So, once you know this about yourself, you can learn to do the opposite. You learn that you need to align with what you like so that you have more enthusiasm for doing it.

When you find those activities where you like yourself and you like what you're doing, a strong, seemingly unending current of energy opens up. This is when time loses meaning, spouses have to pull you away from your desk when it's bedtime and caffeine isn't required because there's nothing else you need to fuel you other than your own internal power source. You get a huge boost of energy from being the best you and doing what you love to do, so the next step towards answering Question 1 is to notice 1) what gives you energy, and 2) what drains your energy.

The things that take your energy are things your intuition is telling you are not a great fit for you; this can include people, places, activities or even types of exercise. On the other hand, things that you just want to do more and more of because they light you up are a signal that you're connected to your source of inner power. What lights you up is like a battery, fuelling your projects and passions and giving you the endurance to become a master of them, because you want to go back to them again and again instead of giving up too soon. When you can feel that you're plugged into your power source, know that you're tuning in to something with potential that's likely to be in tune with your soul purpose.

Feeling disempowered?

When we start to notice that we've been falling out of tune, the way to take back control is by taking radical responsibility for our own lives. This can mean taking drastic leaps, shifts and jumps into what we feel will be more aligned for us, even if our logical brain hasn't caught up yet. Deciding we're going to live in line with our intuition is a decision to accept full responsibility for our own lives because we recognize that we're the source of our own power. By passing the responsibility on to others, we're saying to ourselves that we're not powerful, which can mean that we spend the rest of our lives waiting in frustration for what we know needs to be done.

Each time you turn away from your own insights and ignore your own power, you're demoting your intuition – until eventually it can seem as though you've lost touch with it completely. If you feel disempowered and out of control in one area of your life, it's most likely to be because there's an intuitive signal you haven't yet noticed telling you what's not working for you. One way to test if something is aligned with your power or disempowering you is with muscle testing, also known as applied kinesiology.

Intuition in action: muscle testing

You're literally stronger when something is fully in tune with you. If you're trying to force yourself to behave like someone you're not, then not only will you feel inauthentic to some degree, but it'll make you weaker in terms of both your internal energy supply and your physical ability. Muscle testing works on the basis that you're stronger when something is true for you, and weaker when something isn't. There are various ways you can use muscle testing to check if something is in tune with you or not.

If you have a decision to make and you want a practical way to access your intuition that gives you a clear 'yes' or 'no' based on the intuitive intelligence of your body, stand up and say confidently a series of statements that you know are definitely true or false. For example:

+ 'My name is Liz.'

+ 'I am in England.'

+ 'I am a dog.'

When you say these out loud (or, if that's not possible, in your mind), your body will naturally fall one way – backwards or forwards. These first few statements are a tester, because they'll show you which way you'll swing for 'true' and which way you'll swing for 'false'. Like a human pendulum and the ultimate lie detector, your body will show you whether you really think that something is true or false. Once you've established which way you move for 'yes' and 'no', it's time to start asking the less obvious questions you want to know the answers to.

You can use muscle testing to find out about any hidden beliefs you have, which way you want to go with a certain decision, or how you really feel about something that you haven't yet got clarity on. Just to warn you: the results can be shocking! Your conscious brain might think one thing, but your body might be telling you something else. That's because your intuition speaks through your body and doesn't always match up with the thoughts in your brain, which are generated from a totally different place.

Your intuition is connected with your soul, so it wants you to thrive and feel peaceful and free, whereas your ego is connected with your brain, which wants to keep you safe and alive in your physical form. Awww, the ego isn't such a bad thing... it wants to protect you. However, a substantial amount of work is required to bypass the busy mind to reach those higher levels of heightened intuition, and working with your body is a great way to get started. Your body is an incredible device for knowing what feels in or out of tune for you, and it's very easy to use. The issue is that most people never got an instruction manual and so they never trust what they're feeling.

This way of muscle testing is the simplest, but there are a few other ways that you can research and practise too, such as creating a circle with your thumb and forefinger and seeing how easy it is to break it by pulling the forefinger of your other hand through it. Another one is how strong your arm is when you hold it out and press against it. Again, this shows how you're literally strongest when you're living in tune with your embodied intuition.

It's not selfish to be sovereign

Another thing that might be coming up for you right now is that it's selfish to be sovereign. After all, how many lifetimes have we lived with the belief that we're not the ones with the power? *Not anymore.* When you choose the intuitive way, you're choosing you as your sovereign source of your own happiness, authority and intelligence.

You won't have to accept anyone else's views or opinions any longer if they don't feel authentic and true for you. You are the source of your own wisdom. You are the source of your own power. You are capable of finding your own answers and seeking out your own truths. If that isn't power, I don't know what is...

Accepting how much power you actually have over your own life and your own decisions may be a hard pill to swallow, because yes, it requires radical responsibility. It means you can't blame others for your bad choices, and you can't blame mum and dad for screwing the rest of your life up. Maybe they didn't – maybe you get to choose again. Maybe we're the ones with the power, and maybe our life is our own to guide forwards and make better than it used to be.

If you were the sovereign source of your own power, what would that look like and how would you think differently every day? The most powerful people in the world accept their power as a given and don't shy away from it, probably because they also have lots of other people looking up to them and telling them they're powerful. When we don't have anyone else in awe of us, we have to create our own sense of power. The best way to do that is by staying close to the things that make you feel like the most aligned and authentic version of yourself, which is when you become unstoppable.

Tune in to your own power

If you start from a place of recognizing your own power, life will become a continual process of revealing rather than pursuing. Opportunities will reveal themselves. As you explore more of what you enjoy, you'll discover new parts of yourself and new talents. And then the results will reveal themselves, and you'll know that they're actually aligned with you because you haven't bent yourself out of shape in order to get them. The more you can reveal your own unhindered self, the more powerful you are. When do you see more of your soul self and what does she/he/they feel like? When do you feel like a success rather than like your personal power is being stripped away? What would you choose to do if it was only up to you?

Once you tune in to your power and recognize when the greatest version of you comes out, you'll find where your energy has been hiding all along. You'll feel motivated to keep growing and expanding, rather than hiding away and avoiding changing what you know deep down isn't right for you. You'll find it easy to tune in to what you want across all areas of your life because it simply means following what brings you the most joy. What you find easy – and what fills your power up rather than drains you – really is where you have the potential to change your life and the lives of many others. Gone are the days of needing to push, drag and force yourself into doing things that you don't really want to do just because you feel like you 'should'. What makes you feel like the most natural and unhindered version of you?

These are things to think about when you want to reclaim your power and start to live intuitively. When you decide to develop your intuition, trust is the most important piece – trusting yourself, trusting the information that you get and trusting that you're a worthy enough candidate to receive the message. Believing your own inner guidance more than anyone else's and knowing that you're the one who holds all the power is the very first step towards living an in tune and empowered new life. Your greatest source of energy is somewhere within, and it's by aligning your life with your inner life force that you'll see the full extent of your capability. When you love what you're doing, and you love who you're being, that's how you'll know that you're in tune with the greatest version of you.

Journalling questions to go deeper into Power

🖊 What does the most authentic version of you like to do?

🖊 When do you feel strong and empowered?

🖊 Do you believe that you're responsible for your own life?

Pain

Question 2: Where have you suffered enough to know how to help others?

. . . .

'I don't think of all the misery, but of the beauty that still remains.'

Anne Frank

Great challenges prepare people for great success. If you've lived a life that's led you through pain, a gateway has been opened to take you deeper into yourself and your soul. Without experiencing life fully, you can never experience yourself fully, and pain is a mother that teaches us how to nurture ourselves. By traversing through pain and transcending it, you will eventually be able to see what it taught you – and these are all lessons that you can use to teach and guide others.

When you're in the thick of it, this will be too hard to see, but once you're through to the other side, you'll have a delicate sensitivity to what other people are going through. Past pain that you've experienced has given you a unique intuition that senses what someone else needs to help them heal, and by tuning in to this part of you that was once wounded, you may find a deep sense of purpose here. The next step to connecting with your intuition is understanding that it will be awakened in many ways, not all of which are pleasant.

Your pain is a guide

Travelling through pain is no easy task, and in no way is this to minimize anyone's trauma or life circumstances. There are so many problems across the world today – such as issues of discrimination and inequality – and these are the exact kind of injustices and situations which you might feel an urge to focus your healing work on. You might also feel that the things you've been personally affected by are the most urgent for you to fix and solve, because by doing so, you're justifying your own experience and transforming it. This is no bad thing either – in fact, it's incredibly powerful.

We all want to connect with people who have experienced something similar to us when we're in our time of need, because their guidance can feel more authentic if we know that they've actually been through it and come out the other side. If we can communicate with someone in a way that shows we really understand them, then we could be the one who finally gets through to them and changes their life for the better. This intuitive ability we have to tune in to pain is how we can see clearly into situations in a sensitive and profound way that someone else who hasn't experienced that type of pain would never be able to.

To find out how you have a unique, innate intuition that other people with a different history may not have, you need to be willing to dive deep into the pain you've experienced; only by truly facing it, feeling it and rewriting the narrative of it can you discover the insights it has gifted you. To do this, you may need to work with a licensed therapist, professional healer or expert in the specific type of trauma that you're working through. You can also do the following exercise on your own by connecting to the past version of you who was once in a very different situation.

Intuition in action: inner child work

I have found inner child work to be incredibly powerful. If you suffered pain in childhood, connecting with the version of you at that age enables you to tune in to exactly how the younger version of you felt and what they need. Doing this will mean that you need to devote some time to yourself to cry, feel, release, understand and then integrate.

A good way to start connecting with your younger self is by having a photo of you at the age when you know that things weren't going well in your life. Start by looking into the eyes of that younger you. Tune in to their pain and suffering, and then compare it with your life today to see what has changed. It's likely you may still feel those wounds today, but there are many things that you'll see differently as an adult who's overcome what you were going through then. Let that younger version of you know that they're always supported, loved and held by their primary caregiver who will never leave them or let them down: you as an adult.

Meeting your inner child and connecting with her/him/them regularly will inevitably strengthen your intuition because you're accessing all the lessons, emotions and experiences that life has given you, without keeping old versions of you shut off and separate because there's too much pain in your past to face. When we turn a blind eye to our own pain, we might find ourselves being triggered by it instead of feeling empowered to help people because we know what we've overcome ourselves, and how. This 'how' is the important piece that could be a part of your purpose. To recognize and resonate with what you see in others through your intuition, you first need to recognize the full range of everything you've felt before.

Trauma is a teacher

Developing your intuition by seeing through pain in this way not only allows you to guide other people when they're struggling through a storm, but will also help you to see more clearly through one of yours next time the sea starts to swell in your life. It's important to remember that no one starts by seeing pain as an enormous growth and learning opportunity. It's not something we will ever welcome gladly into our life because we're humans who are wired to seek pleasure and avoid pain at all costs, but once we've sailed through pain a few times and found our own sense of calm again, we just get more skilled at navigating it.

My first real experience of trauma was the break-up of my family when I was nine years old. The day we all moved out of our home to go our separate ways is drawn on my mind in permanent ink. As I stepped out of the front door for the last time, uncertainty ran through me like water through the bricks of the broken home I was walking away from. Rain was beating down around me and all over me, but I didn't care – or notice – as I stopped to turn back for one last look at the house that I'd lived in and loved. The bin bag full of toys that had been thrown together at the last minute was weighing more and more heavily in my arms each second I stood there, until I had no choice but to run through the puddles on the pavement and hurl myself into the car with it. My dad was waiting at the wheel to take me away, and it couldn't wait. It was time for another family to start their attempt at a happy home there.

The uncertainty that penetrated my life and home throughout childhood conceived an anxiety within me that would one day trigger my quest to try and find certainty in understanding. It was my greatest pain which forced me to find the answers that I now know – and can share to help heal the pain of others. The Universe was delivering me a gift, but I couldn't see what it was until I'd walked far enough away from it and could see it in full view from a distance. Up close it was too big, too overwhelming, too hard to see the whole picture. Pain does pass, and when it does, it leaves us with new lessons, new strength and a new perspective; a piece of a puzzle that other people are looking for to complete theirs. When you understand your own puzzle, you have the chance to share your final picture of how it all fits together with others, to give them hope that they'll get to the end too one day. The route to healing that you couldn't quite put your finger on once upon a time could be the route you're here to guide others down.

Client case study: addiction to inspiration

When I started working with Chantelle, the first things that struck me were her stunning bright green eyes and warm, cosy energy, which said without speaking that she put others first and cared deeply about their feelings. The next was her story. Like all of the people who came to work with me as coaching clients, she felt that spirituality was calling her – to the point where working in anything else was starting to feel more and more unfulfilling as the days and weeks went on. We all have a story and a history, and when we leverage them in the right way, we can use them to create a huge amount of good. This is what I began to work on with Chantelle.

During her 20s, she'd overcome years of alcohol addiction and substance abuse, managing to get through the other side into her 30s completely sober. Like a lot of people who have overcome enormous adversity and found their inner strength, a spiritual transformation had begun, and – like a butterfly from a chrysalis – she was finally ready to fly and show her true colours. A career in spiritual coaching was the perfect fit for Chantelle because, as I've explained in this chapter, exploring the depths of pain, depression, anxiety and loss creates a deep empathy and intuitive sensitivity that can't be learned from a textbook.

We focused on the transformation element of her new coaching offering and she was so brave to start sharing her story with a vulnerability and raw integrity not often seen on Instagram. Through her bravery and willingness to create change, she's since been featured in The Times newspaper and now inspires others – whether they have a history of addiction or not – with her story of healing and the sense of purpose that she's found on her spiritual journey.

Intuition in the dark

We often need someone to light the way through pain because, when we're in the midst of it, our intuition is clouded by the dark, dense emotions that we're feeling. When we've been shaken by a profound sense of loss, or are blinded by anger and rage, these intense emotions form a thick fog around our intuition. While we're busy fully embodying this human experience, the wisdom of our soul will take a back seat – but when we're ready to tune in again, it'll be there waiting to tell us the lesson. This isn't a bad thing, as we all need to experience pain fully to move through it, but this is when the advice of people who have gone through the same adversity before comes in handy.

To solve this sense of separation that the illusion of losing your intuition can create, we all have to try and trust, regardless. Again, this is something that gets easier over time – like when you've gone through enough divine detours to know that one day you'll look back and see how everything worked out perfectly in the end. After going through this a few times, you feel safer trusting that things are working in your favour and that you're still being guided, even if it's a route you didn't see yourself going down. Keeping the faith through pain will allow you to see the lessons that you're meant to learn sooner; and the sooner you learn, the sooner you can use them to help others.

Your pain can have a purpose

Regardless of how it feels, your pain doesn't have to be the end of you. In fact, it can be a way to find purpose and meaning if you choose to use it as such. You're the expert in a certain type of suffering that will resonate with other people and you can help to give them hope until they come out the other side. As personal as pain feels when we're in the thick of it, we're not the only ones to suffer it. That's why there are charities, support groups and AA meetings to help people come together in their pain. Instead of it being something that separates you from others, pain can actually be a unifying force, as long as you're prepared to share your story.

Many spiritual authors before me have adopted this perspective that pain can be turned into purpose, which is why we write about our stories and what we've learned in the hope that it will help others to see the gift of their own unique life journeys. I'm so thankful for the times when I cried and when I felt so dark that I couldn't even cry, because now I can empathize with others. When I write and teach, it's with the aim of delivering a gift of healing – and I know that it wouldn't be possible if I didn't have depth carved into me at an early age from the fast and aggressive rivers of change that ravaged every part of my life. If you're a wounded healer too, then you'll understand what I mean and your soul is probably nodding along right now.

When we're searching for ways to soothe our own emotional wounds, we can find cures that could change the world. I don't know what your own experiences of pain have been, but I know that they'll have taught you something. Your journey to healing gave you the exact solution that someone, somewhere, is looking for right now. By leading and guiding them with your truth and your message, you might be able to get them to a place where they can then do the same for someone else. It's a ripple effect. You're the pebble that was thrown into the water once.

By intuitively leading ourselves through our suffering and asking the pain 'what do you want to teach me?', we'll uncover the way it works as a cosmic catalyst for change and growth. If we open ourselves up to see the possibilities our pain has provided – such as a way for us to feel more purpose and meaning by helping others – then we can prime ourselves for finding the positives in anything. Our most formidable opponent in times of pain will always be our brain, whose sole (not soul) purpose is to protect its physical life, not to see the good in it. Feel your way through any fear in your brain by asking yourself: 'How did I grow through this? What did I learn? And how much stronger have the bad times made me?'

When we decide to view the pain we've experienced in our lives as a lesson that can help and heal others, we'll feel the joy of knowing that we've made a positive impact. By alchemizing our own experience in this way, we not only help other people, but we can also find peace within ourselves. Everything weaves together in sacred serendipity to give us the tools that we need to complete our mission in the world. So, where have you suffered enough to know how to help others?

Without the wisdom we gain from dealing with these events, we'd never know what other people need to get them out of mentally, emotionally and spiritually painful situations. Try not to keep your realizations to yourself if you have the chance to help others. You can be the light leader, the proof pain ends and the ray of hope. What you've overcome can be another way to unlock your intuition, as between the deeper layers of your human experience, seeds were planted within you to one day bloom into beautiful moments of realization.

Journalling questions to go deeper into Pain

✎ What was your biggest trauma, and how has it changed you?

✎ What route to healing do more people need to know about?

✎ How can you give your pain a purpose?

Problem

Question 3: If you could solve one problem in the world, what would it be?

....

'Somewhere inside all of us is the
power to change the world.'

Roald Dahl

How you align your priorities of what's important to you with your daily life is a huge piece of what will make you feel as though you're living either in tune or out of tune. Your intuition will pull you towards the problems that mean the most to you, like an internal navigation system pointing you towards the way you can go next to find your sense of purpose. Whatever your own priorities are, as long as you know them and live by them, you'll find it much easier to keep living in tune with your intuition.

What problems do you feel pulled towards?

To find out what your priorities are in terms of the problems that you see in the world, sit down with your journal and start brainstorming. Start to think about all the things in the world that you'd solve if you could, and allow your soul to speak over your ego if it comes up with any reasons why you shouldn't write things down. Whether you write a bullet-point list or a spider diagram with the word 'Problems' in the middle and all your ideas scattered around it, you'll start to see that there are quite a few things you have a desire to solve. This page will look different for everyone, but for each person, it's full of purpose and likely to be influenced by some personal experience of pain.

Next, after you've written down everything you can possibly think of, try to empty your mind and tune in to the problem you're most drawn to. It may be the first one you wrote down, or a single overarching problem that's the connecting link between a few of the issues you've listed. Undoubtedly, your intuition will pull you towards one problem more than any others on the page, because you think that solving this specific issue would have a greater impact overall than solving some of the others.

When you feel yourself zooming in on a particular problem, it's your intuition telling you that it's important for you to look at. Without being able to see it in the first place, you'd never be able to solve it – and if something is glaringly obvious to you, then it's attracting your attention for a reason. Like a cosmic command telling you where to go next, the reason could be that solving this particular problem will be where you'll find the most satisfaction and fulfilment.

As uncomfortable as it can be to look at problems, if we didn't see them then we'd stay blind to them, passing them by with no sense of passionate purpose about how we can improve the world. Many people find their calling here, hidden in the problem they most want to pull apart. It could be the same for you, which is why understanding your answer to Question 3 is so useful. Whether it's something that's affected you personally or not, the sign that something about it is resonating with you is how much it irritates you into action. When something triggers you, you can use it as a signal to see if you're living in tune with your true values and priorities.

Your problems, your priorities

Knowing your priorities is what will allow you to assess intuitively where you are now and where you're going, so that you always know if you're living in tune. A useful model that helps us to understand this is Maslow's hierarchy of needs[1], which highlights that we have a hierarchy of values, a hierarchy of what we think of as problems and a hierarchical list of what we think we need.

Figure 1: Maslow's hierarchy of needs

The basis of Maslow's model is that only once our base needs have been met can we start focusing on our higher, more evolved needs. To show how this works, the model is illustrated by an upwards-pointing triangle striped with horizontal layers running up it. The layers are stacked on top of each other because, as we move upwards through the layers of this virtual triangle, what we see as the biggest problem in our life will change.

On the first layer, along the bottom of the triangle, are our physical needs, which means that our initial instinct is always going to be to make sure that we have enough food and shelter by being able to pay our rent and other monthly outgoings. We need to keep our physical bodies alive as our top priority, otherwise we're no good to anyone.

Once those needs are fulfilled, we might feel ready to start focusing on the next layers: our emotional needs, psychological needs and spiritual needs. After everything else has been satisfied, we can turn our attention towards the top layer of the triangle, which is our need to reach our full potential, known as self-actualization. Knowing this model is so helpful because it goes a long way towards explaining why we all focus on different things...

When we're struggling financially, of course we're going to focus more on just getting by and making sure we have enough money for ourselves and our family to survive each month. In tougher times, we're much less likely to invest the majority of our energy into solving global problems, because that's not where we see the biggest issue before us today, tomorrow and next week. We always need to figure out how to survive first.

So, it's important that we don't judge people for not caring about the exact same issues that we do, because they're in a totally different situation to us. Understanding our own priorities is important but, as much as possible, we should try to respect other people's priorities too, because they're living totally different lives and might need to solve their own problems before they can turn their attention to anyone else.

Understanding your unique values

Those who already have all their physical needs fully met, and are living abundant lives emotionally and financially, might feel more inclined to start looking outwards and seeing what else they can solve instead. This is why so many people who end up in well-paid office jobs are staring out of the window all day and realizing that they want so much more than just money. If this is you, it's very important to start looking around at how exactly you're feeling most called to help. In fact, I'd go as far as saying that, for those of us who have our personal needs abundantly met, it's our *responsibility* to start focusing on these other things, so that we're moving the world forwards to support everyone and not just ourselves.

I identify a lot with how this triangle works, because it was only once I got to a certain point of space and ease, knowing that money wasn't the most important thing for me anymore (because thanks to a corporate career in my 20s I actually had some), that my attention shifted to something else. That's when the search for meaning really started. So, if you're reading this and the thought of having to solve other people's problems when you haven't even got capacity to solve your own yet is stressing you out, please don't feel guilty or overwhelmed.

It may be that you spend most of your time thinking about your own problems, but that could be for a reason too – because the way you get yourself out of them will be a way that you can soon share to help other people who are where you used to be.

Other examples of the sorts of problems you may notice might include, for example, a lack of support for people with disabilities, such as the need for more services for the hearing-impaired to help deaf people navigate more easily through a society geared towards hearing people. Or you might be seeing that divorce seems to be an epidemic around you, and you know how much more help is needed for people who struggle to keep their relationship standing through life events such as grief, miscarriage and financial strain. Or in my case, I can see that people are spiritually disconnected, not listening to their intuition, and lacking a sense of meaning and purpose in their everyday life.

My lovely mother, as another example, is an OAP eco-warrior who (having learned how to use a laptop later in life) now sends me, my brother and my sister a link to every Greenpeace petition going. Hell hath no fury like my mother seeing a tree being cut down... she'll fly into a rage and has no qualms about confronting someone for felling a defenceless tree. She's also been known to storm out of the house in nothing but her nightdress to yell at a woman because she was sitting in her car and leaving the engine running. One Christmas, she bought my five-year-old niece a high-vis jacket, gloves and litter-picker to use on one of their trips down to the local beach to pick up plastic. Environmental issues are definitely the number one problem she'd most like to solve in the world.

Intuition in action: living in tune with your values

One of the first exercises I ask my coaching clients to complete is a priority list of their values. This is because knowing your values is what will make the difference between being stuck in a life that feels totally uncomfortable and out of alignment rather than one which feels like the perfect fit for you. If you don't know what problems are *your* priorities, you're far more likely to be influenced by other people to help them solve theirs, even when those may not be in tune for you.

For some people, having a stable office job until reaching retirement age could be the worst thought imaginable, because their number one value is freedom and their number two value is adventure. For others, however, it could be the best thing in the world, if their number one value is stability and their number two value is security. As I've explained, I do believe this exercise also helps to minimize judgement, because it helps us to know ourselves deeply – and the more we know ourselves, the more we're able to see other people clearly without judgement, because we're not projecting our own frustrations onto them.

Your values are unique and serve a purpose because they allow you to live as the most authentic version of you. To find out what they are, grab your journal and write down this list:

✦ Freedom

✦ Adventure

✦ Growth

✦ Stability

- ✦ Wealth

- ✦ Relationships

- ✦ Impact

- ✦ Status

- ✦ Resilience

- ✦ Security

- ✦ Loyalty

- ✦ Harmony

Then, sit quietly for two minutes and try to keep your mind as empty of thoughts as possible. Look at the page and, without questioning which ones you're most drawn to, put 1 next to your top priority on the list, followed by numbers 2, 3, 4, etc. You may struggle to rank one value above another if two have the same level of importance for you, in which case you could give them both the same ranking.

Once you've numbered them all, rewrite the list of values in order of their importance to you. Keep this list somewhere you can always refer to it – whether that's at the front of your journal, in your office or on your fridge. Being super clear on your values and priorities will keep you in tune with your intuition so you can make life choices that keep you on track.

Beware: when you do this exercise, you may notice how much judgement you have around your own values and priorities. Judgement gets in the way of understanding because it's our fearful and conditioned ego telling us what we 'should' be thinking and wanting, rather than the truth of what our soul really wants – which our intuition is always trying to point us towards. One is more subtle than the other. Your intuition is more likely to appear as a feeling, whereas your conditioning and judgement are more likely to show up in the internal dialogue that's always happening in your mind.

....

I'll keep reiterating this point until the metaphorical cows come home: your intuition will always be limited by conflicting thoughts of what you 'should' do, and the same is true for this exercise (as with all in this book). To truly awaken your intuition, you need to be prepared to pass through any judgement and conditioning in your mind; to be honest with yourself – without outside influence – about what you're really feeling and what you're really drawn to.

By understanding what your values are, you can prioritize your life accordingly. If you're spending your time attending to the problems that are actually most important to you, you're likely to feel a strong sense of purpose by being part of the solution. If you don't know or are misaligned with your values, that's when your intuition will start to tell you that you're out of tune. You'll have a sense that your time is being wasted or could be better spent elsewhere, even if you don't quite know how yet. You might be feeling bitterness or frustration, which can sometimes bubble up to the point where you're lashing out at the people you love. You might even feel completely lost because you don't even know what your values are, and therefore you're living totally out of tune with them. Your priorities are within you for a purpose, so it's absolutely essential that you know what your values are in order to live led by your intuition rather than other people's expectations.

When it comes to this topic in particular, judgement can be rife, because everyone has such strong opinions about the problems in the world. Rightly so, but that still mustn't stop you following what *your* deepest calling is and the problems that *you* most want to solve. This is where you'll be most effective. This is where your intuition is guiding you towards. This is where you can have the most impact, and this is where you'll be living in tune, because you'll be aware of what's really important to you and what your soul is here to do.

Journalling questions to go deeper into Problem

🖉 What type of suffering stands out to you the most?

🖉 Which root issue could lead to the biggest change if it was solved?

🖉 What do you wish you had the cure for?

Panorama

Question 4: What solution can you see clearly that other people can't?

....

'If the challenge exists, so must the solution.'

Rona Mlnarik

We all have the power to solve problems because we have a gift that I call 'panorama vision', which is the ability to see things in a way that other people can't. Sometimes, we don't even realize how unique the solutions we see are because they clearly make sense to us – but without actually sharing them and putting them into action, these solutions may never make their way out into the world. When solutions stay stuck inside us due to our own hesitancy about being bold and breathing life into them, part of *us* will also stay stuck.

If you're being drawn towards a certain issue, you probably also have a deep desire in your soul to fix it. Finding out what this is for you might happen through a light-bulb moment of inspiration, a dream you have one night or a problem you're forced to find a solution to in your own life. It might not always be simple or straightforward to put into action, but when you tune in to what you want to fix, you'll be guided to take the first step, which will lead on to the next, and then the next. Trusting your inner knowing is a process, but once you do, you'll start to see how your intuition is always offering you a unique perspective on how to help solve problems in the world and in your own life.

Soul solutions

Your imagination is the lens through which you'll be able to see and receive creative solutions to any problems you're facing right now. We all download new ideas in this way, which is why they might not make sense to anyone else at first; no one else can see them while they're still in your own imagination. Through your intuition you'll get ideas to give you the answers you've been looking for, as well as the solutions to problems in the wider world – possibly the exact same problems you've realized you're most drawn to solving in the last chapter. When you get an unexplained sense of a solution that could help someone, it's vital that you pay attention and honour yourself as a sacred source of guidance and wisdom.

An intuitive idea may not make logical sense, but it could feel amazing and full of promise to you and, as the person experiencing the idea, you also need to trust the feelings that come along with it. You might need to ride the emotional wave until the initial buzz of excitement from an 'Aha' moment dies down, or wait for the idea to unfold slowly, until you can see fully how it's going to be the solution you need. With every impulsive insight that drops in, which you feel a need to share, a new potential reality opens up too – one in which you have the chance to make an inimitable imprint on the world.

Trusting your intuition

What often holds us back from bringing our solutions out into the world is the same thing that holds us back from following our intuition at all: not having enough faith and confidence in ourselves to trust it. The vision you see clearly in your imagination is a roadmap for you to follow and, first of all, you need to trust what you're seeing inside your mind enough to know how valuable your vision is. Unfortunately, as human beings, we've entrenched ourselves in the shared belief that other people are better, more worthy and more qualified than us to sort things out. This is a huge crisis when it comes to solving things because all the greatest ideas come initially from a spark of inspiration. Those who have made the biggest difference in the world trusted their inspiration implicitly and then acted on it.

For example, Albert Einstein is known as the father of modern physics, so you might assume that intuition would be in opposition to his scientific work. However, the truth is that he was actually heavily reliant on his unique outlook for answers, saying: 'the gift of imagination has meant more to me than any talent for absorbing absolute knowledge... all great achievements of science must start from intuitive knowledge.'[2] Every solution – scientific or otherwise – started from an idea that rose up in someone's imagination from their intuition. Having confidence in your unique vision and trusting that it's important is all you need to start a new solution, and in the words of Einstein: 'I believe in intuition and inspiration... at times I feel certain I am right while not knowing the reason.'

Intuition in action: inspiration inventory

As an intuitive entrepreneur and spiritual author, I've made a living by following my intuition and providing solutions to people's spiritual problems. The process of catching and trusting your intuition is something you can get better at with practice, so here's how to start practising...

Designate a small notepad as your 'inspiration pad', to be used only for taking an inventory of all your intuitive ideas. I specifically suggest a small one – ideally around A6 size – so that you can carry it with you at all times in your bag, coat pocket or car. Oh, and of course you'll need a pen to go with it too!

This exercise seems simple, but it's actually an extremely powerful way of testing whether you trust your intuition enough to get your inspiration pad out all the time and write down each intuitive nudge that comes up. Whenever you feel any of the following, add them to your inspiration inventory:

✦ When you feel like you can predict what's going to happen

✦ When you have a random thought, phrase or idea that seems as though it's dropped into your head out of nowhere, rather than being part of your mind's monologue

✦ When you wake up from a dream and feel like there was a meaningful message in there for you (for example, guidance forwards, a message from a passed loved one or a vision of what's going to happen)

I also like to put a date by each of my entries so that I can look back through past journals and see which of my predictions came true. This will prove to you with undeniable evidence the power of your own intuition, and it'll also mean you don't forget any of the amazing ideas you get. I know that in my experience the true intuitive ideas that drop in can vanish as quickly as they appeared, at which point I'm left kicking myself because by not writing it down I missed the perfect name for a course or masterclass. Save yourself the frustration by adding to your inspiration inventory every time your intuition tells you something.

It will help you to distinguish your intuition from your regular thoughts and it'll provide indisputable proof of how powerful your intuition can really be. Honouring your intuition with this exercise will strengthen it, as you're placing more value on it by showing that you're ready to listen and take notes.

As you start documenting your intuitive insights, you'll start to find out how incredibly random they are. This might be exactly why you've discounted them before, shrugging them off and moving on, only to find weeks later that one of the ideas was the exact thing you should have followed through with. Once this has happened often enough, hopefully it feels safer to follow the random nudges – but I know it can be scary to follow inspiration alone, so another thing that you can do to confirm any ideas you have is ask for external signs.

Following your guidance

In 2019, I decided to move to Glastonbury on a total whim, guided only by my intuition and a desire to experiment with it. This small old English town in the south-west of the country started calling to something within me even though I'd never been before, because I'd heard rumours that it had more spiritual classes, people and bookshops than you could shake a smudge stick at. I wanted to meet and connect with other spiritual people, and while I was there I learned a lot of lessons about this special community, which is shrouded in a cloud of mysticism and biodegradable glitter. It's indeed a community, as I found from living in a place with so much mythical legend that people from all over the world travel there to experience new levels of quirkiness and the undeniable energy that the town has. It's steeped in mythology and tales of Merlin, with a rich culture of paganism. As a friend once said, in Glastonbury 'it's easier to buy crystals than socks'. All of this attracts a certain type of person.

I've always considered myself 'half and half': semi-spiritual and semi-practical, sometimes leaning more into one side than the other in different parts of my life. Ethereal, esoteric ideas alone rarely interest me unless there's some kind of practical, tangible application, and because of this I always had trouble feeling as though I fully fitted into either world. I was too spiritual for the 'normal' world that most people live in, but wasn't fitting fully into the spiritual community I'd found myself in at Glastonbury either. One day, when I was feeling like a lonely walking dichotomy, I asked for a sign.

This is a common thing I'll do when I need confirmation or clarity, and I definitely recommend doing the same when you're in a similar situation. Even if you don't believe that it comes from some external force, it can help you to clarify your own ideas of what you do or don't actually want. So, I asked for a sign: 'Universe… if I'm meant to be both and that's my unique path to walk, please confirm.' Then I let go and let it be. When you ask for a sign, it's important to forget that you asked and release your request, knowing that if it's meant to be then the sign will appear at the perfect moment. Over the next few weeks, I started to think about how I could blend my love of both spirituality and business together in order to create a new coaching offering that felt totally aligned and in tune for me. My request for a sign had completely vanished from my mind – until one showed up.

It was delivered through my friend and soul sister, Rachel Alyce, who shared a picture on her social media of a card that she'd pulled for her audience from Yasmin Boland's *Moonology Oracle Cards* deck: 'Full Moon in Pisces: balance spirituality and practicality.' She'd taken a photo of this message and the stars had aligned for me to see it at the perfect moment. It was shared for everyone in her audience, but the words still seemed to speak directly to my soul. The message on this card embodied exactly what I was feeling called to express through blending together the two opposing sides of myself to create an individual offering with my name on it.

I knew that I was meant to be both, and that I was meant to stand between the two worlds and bring them closer together. More than anything, I wanted everything I'd learned about spirituality to benefit the mainstream world, and I also wanted everything I'd learned in the mainstream world to benefit the spiritual world. I wanted to blend the best of both, even though I couldn't see anyone around me offering the same combination of principles that I felt deeply drawn to: intuition, entrepreneurship and coaching – all with a spiritual twist, of course. It was only when I started offering this and showcasing my whole mix of talents and passions without dimming them down – even if they didn't logically seem to fit – that I started to find money, success and soulmate clients. If we're not being fully ourselves, we'll never attract the people who perfectly fit us and are in tune with our idiosyncrasies.

Turn intuition into action

It takes practice to trust your inspiration, but when you do, it'll reveal to you the full power of your intuition. When you're searching for an answer or stuck about what to do next, notice any ideas that drop into your head when you're not expecting them. Solutions from your soul will come to you in random moments and, with the gift of a unique vision that you have from all of your life experiences so far, you'll get to see things differently, and your intuition will guide you towards specific ways that you can 'soul-ve' things differently.

What your soul shows you through your imagination and intuition could be completely different to what anyone else has thought to offer before. How many solutions are still in people's minds because they haven't tuned in to their intuition yet, or trusted their random sparks of unexplained inspiration? The way your viewpoint is different could be exactly what someone else needs to make a positive change in their life. In your own life, you may already see the right solution you need, but not be taking action on it yet. If this is you, and you haven't got confidence in the answer that part of you knows is what you need to do right now, ask for a sign and see what appears. Once intuition turns into action, you can start to make your mark on the world by owning your place in it as the only one of you.

Journalling questions to go deeper into Panorama

✐ When do you thrive at solving problems creatively?

✐ How do you see things differently to everyone else?

✐ What is your vision of a better world?

Pioneer

Question 5: In what unique way can you move the world forwards?

....

'The number one reason people fail in life is because they listen to their friends, family and neighbours.'

Napoleon Hill

Your soul knows who you are, but do you? Outside influences can be so compelling that you follow them instead, forgetting yourself in the process. Everyone is different, but sacred in their own way. By owning your uniqueness and confidently choosing yourself over the crowd, you'll align with your soul-centred power and make way for the part of you that is capable of creating real change.

The best route for you may not be the regular route, and you'll need to make peace with that if you're really committed to living in tune. We all have individual ways we can move the world forwards if we fully follow our intuition, and if you're prepared to stand out and lead the way in whatever direction you feel called, the change that you create in the world might reward you with a deep sense of purpose. The most renowned pioneers went after their own crazy ideas and big dreams even when no one else went before them. To make the ultimate impact means ultimately to trust your intuition.

Your individual imprint

When we put other people's ideas and opinions of us before our own intuition, it's a one-way ticket to feeling out of tune. The way we can get back to living in tune is by realizing that we're different, and accepting that it's our individuality that makes us special. Even if not all of us are destined to be radical revolutionaries who are here to make the world spin in a different direction, that doesn't mean merging into the crowd is the next best option. Our compulsion to fit in can hold us back hugely from following our intuition, because the fear of stepping out and being different becomes so overwhelming that it consumes any hope we have of being in alignment with our own sense of personal purpose.

What your soul came here to do is to make an invaluable imprint on the world as the only one of you. So, it's very possible that you're here to be the first one in some way and to bring something new to the table. What you're here to deliver as your *dharma* will vary wildly from person to person. You might be the pioneer in some way in your circle of friends, or you might be the first one in your family to do something different, like going to university. Your business may offer something new to the marketplace, or you might choose a brand-new relationship dynamic, despite what other people around you think of it. There's no denying that it can be hard to bring out the pioneering side of your own spirit, but by doing things for you, for what you find fun and for what you enjoy, you'll automatically become magnetic and people will start to notice.

Remember that we all have a sphere of influence. The size of our sphere is different from person to person, but we still have one, so we can use ours to create the type of change that we feel called to make. We're often inspired most by those who are simply being themselves and that's what we'll find starting to happen when we own our place on Earth authentically as the only one of us.

The imprint you make on people isn't always obvious, but with each impression you leave, you're also putting your individual mark on the world as a whole. You *are* influential even as an individual, despite what you may have been led to believe before. Your individuality is where you'll have integrity and it's the ultimate commitment to honesty – both to yourself and with everyone else.

It's easier to walk the familiar way, which is why so many people do it; it's signposted, with good reviews and a guaranteed outcome. What's not to love? Yet when you feel tempted to stay the same and fit in, look around you and see if you really want what everyone else has. When you follow the wrong crowd, you lose control over the destination you're heading towards. To decide your own destination and end result, you need to choose your own way forwards and continue on that way despite any discomfort you feel as a result of being different.

The successful pioneer

The role of a pioneer is not to follow what's been done before and do what they already know works; pioneers are those who tread a new path without knowing where it ends or what surprises might be in store for them along the way. It requires a steady appetite for risk to become a successful pioneer, as well as an enormous amount of belief in the purpose behind what they're pursuing. However, everything great that's ever been created or achieved up until now has required pioneering spirits to make it happen. Otherwise, we'd never know about the invaluable things they've discovered and we wouldn't be benefitting from what we take for granted today: light bulbs, boats, planes, electricity, X-rays – the list goes on. Through being willing to take risks, be innovative and be the first in their field to do something, the pioneers who have gone before us have initiated enormous change.

Their desire to create this change and do things that have never been done before will have arisen from some deep intuitive calling within them, telling them that *they* needed to be the original pioneer. When a similar calling arises within you, giving it a shot – whether other people are on board or not – is the only way to appease your intuition. There is only one way to find out if something will work. You'll never know how you could be brilliant if you never try. You'll never know what you could achieve if you don't begin. And you'll never be a pioneer if you listen to everyone who's just doing what's been done before. Going into space is just as possible as driving a car, or talking to someone on the other side of the world by holding a small piece of metal to your ear. Not too many lifetimes ago, all these things would have been considered laughable because people thought they were impossible...

People laugh at things that they don't know and don't understand because sometimes it isn't their job to understand. Tuning out the noise is sometimes just as important as tuning in, because being too scared of judgement, failure or rejection by other people has killed more dreams than a little bit of gumption ever did. If it's your purpose and your mission, it's *your* job to understand that it feels right for you, and *your* job to do something different to everyone around you. What would you choose to do differently if you could, and how are you being called to move the world forwards in your own unique way?

Client case study: standing out to outstanding

When Kori started working with me, she was well aware that she had a gift, but unsure how to share it. As anyone who's gone through their spiritual awakening and accessed the deepest depths of their intuition will know, it's an unsettling experience. You feel like the odd one out, navigating a completely different reality to everyone else. With a new gift also comes the weight of a burden, knowing that you have extra insights and healing abilities for a purpose, but not knowing how to share them or where to begin – let alone what your friends and family will think when you announce that you're going to create a spiritually aligned life and business that's in direct contradiction with their materialist and/ or religious beliefs. Like so many of my clients, this was exactly why Kori came to me for help.

There was something that made Kori's story special, which is why I wanted to include it here. She was a pioneer in more than just the sense of challenging the status quo by embodying her full spiritual self – she was also born completely deaf. While we worked together, the same limiting belief kept coming up: that it was going to be so much harder to build a business because of her hearing challenges. The huge success she created with her Tarot and Reiki business made me even more sure of this lesson that I want to share with you: sometimes, seeming to be the only one doing something is the most powerful thing of all, with the potential to access untapped avenues of abundance.

Of course, Kori wasn't the only deaf person in the world offering spiritual services, but it certainly seemed as though she was in the minority compared to most people in her line of work, who were hearing. What I told her was that she had a whole community to serve – people who weren't yet being reached by someone speaking their language. Thanks to teaching and giving readings in sign language, her business instantly took off, and her brand has been growing ever since.

The way you think *you're* different is how you can identify with all the other people who feel different in the exact same way, creating a strong bond of loyalty and understanding. In a business sense, the more unique you are, the less competition you have. Owning your offering as something different to what's been available before can end up being a route to reaching the most people and having the most profound impact.

....

Intuition in action: oracle cards

Choosing to put yourself out there as the only one of you because you're following your intuition can definitely feel scary and overwhelming, so the good news is that there are tools you can use to give yourself confidence, direction and support while you're pioneering your own path. I'm a huge advocate of using cards for guidance, and I pull an oracle card for myself first thing every morning. Whenever I have a decision to make, I'll see what Tarot has to say about it, and I've done thousands of card readings for people during my career. This means I've been asked countless times for advice about choosing a deck and using cards for guidance, so here it is...

The first thing you need to do is choose your deck. Assuming you don't yet own one, start by noticing what decks other people are using and, if you feel drawn to one, ask them who it's by. You can also go into a metaphysical shop or search for 'oracle card decks' online and simply use your intuition to guide you. Whichever deck stands out and makes you interested enough to pick it up (or click on it if you're online) is already a strong contender. If none of them are standing out for you, don't feel compelled to just buy one anyway – set the intention that the right deck is going to cross your path at the right time.

There are different types of decks to be aware of: oracle cards and angel cards will be uplifting and full of lovely positive messages; Tarot, on the other hand, is not for the faint-hearted. I love Tarot cards, but they do have the potential to ruin your day, so I wouldn't recommend pulling one for yourself first thing! That said, it's the 'negative' cards within Tarot that allow you to use it for yes/no guidance. When you've chosen your deck (or decks) of choice, cleanse it with an energy-clearing method and connect it to you by holding it to your heart or looking at each individual card and seeing how you relate to it.

To get your guidance, simply shuffle the deck with the question in mind that you want to ask. Naturally stop shuffling when it feels right, and split the deck without thinking too hard about it. The card on top is your answer. Whenever you're facing fear and uncertainty – such as whether you're doing the right thing by doing something different – the message you pull out on a card can be exactly what you need to keep going. Alternatively, the cards can confirm what your intuition is telling you when it's indicating that something is a bad idea but you need an external message to make you really pay attention. I think they're so helpful for when you're going your own way because they can give you clear, concrete messages of support in those moments when you feel uncertain.

Go your own way

If you want to be the same as everyone else, it's probably not a good idea to follow your intuition. The paths it leads you down can be unexpected and uncomfortable if much of your comfort is found from fitting in. Radically following your own guidance will teach you to go your own way. Whatever the little pioneer inside you is saying doesn't have to be completely earth-shattering and ground-breaking – like Thomas Edison inventing the light bulb or Steve Jobs creating the iPhone. The most important thing is that you're not denying your intuition the chance to go your own way, because if you let yourself be led by the need to fit in, you can lose yourself somewhere between the crowd and a need for approval.

You can lead yourself if you believe enough in the importance of what you're doing. By feeling the force of determination that comes from finding out what space you're here to fill, you can overcome any obstacles that might stand between you and your individuality; you can knock down anything that doesn't fit with enough reason for why you're going your own way.

The issue is that this pioneering spirit we all have can get suppressed when we feel threatened by the fear of being laughed at or judged, because other people don't think that we're allowed to be a pioneer. A human part of our mind thinks that it's not safe to be different and that it's a safer bet to be the same. This is part of our primitive mindset, which tries to keep us alive by keeping us as part of the herd – so we can't blame it – but it's important that we follow our deeper feeling of purpose rather than letting outdated fears fence us in.

By knowing how you're unique, you'll also know exactly how you're special. Whether it's seen by other people or not, the way that you shine best is when your soul is singing its own song. Being a pioneer isn't the easy route, but it may be the intuitive route if it's what you feel called to do. Being unique is how you'll have the biggest impact, so even when everyone else seems to be going in a different direction, keep going your own way until you reach a destination you really love.

Journalling questions to go deeper into Pioneer

🖋 If you were to revolutionize one thing, what would it be?

🖋 What would you do differently to everyone else?

🖋 How can you start something that would create change for a better future?

Protest

Question 6: What are you willing to fight for?

....

'The future depends on what we do in the present.'

Mahatma Gandhi

We live in an incredible age, with access to technology, social media and hashtags. Think of the #MeToo movement and think of #BlackLivesMatter (BLM). By just hitting 'post' on Twitter or Instagram, you could start a chain reaction that reaches around the world and into millions of hearts and minds. You never know what change you might create if you step out and share what you believe in, while being guided by a strong sense of hope for what's possible. You can be an agent of change for whatever you think would make the world a better place, and the action you take could end up having an enormous impact.

Listening to your intuition allows you to find your rightful place in whatever movement or change you're meant to create. Even if it's just to change one person's attitude towards something, big or small, all that matters is that you know what you're willing to fight for and what's truly important to you, so you can align your time and energy with doing something about it. This is how you'll live in tune with the part of you that feels like your soul can't fully rest until you start to see some real change in this area.

Create lasting change

When we believe in something strongly and have faith in a purpose greater than us, we can begin to align ourselves with a cause that adds meaning to our lives through the change we make in other people's lives. With the gift of our sensitive and soul-aligned intuition, we're able to tune in to our instincts for what we need to do about it. That feeling of being out of tune with the change we want to create deep down is what can drive us to make a difference. What we want to fight for could be the deep sense of purpose that inspires us to keep moving and progressing – we just need to figure out what it is that we feel so certain about defending, protecting or changing.

This definitely doesn't mean that you need to act out of alignment if your most authentic personality is more inclined to be a peacekeeper and mediator than an aggressive or outspoken person. Whatever your personality and natural inclination, there's still something you believe in so strongly that you know the world would be better for knowing it too. For example, when it comes to spirituality, I'll fight through whatever challenges, limitations or setbacks arise in order to reach my goal of helping people all over the world reconnect with their souls, because I believe it's a fundamental shift that would change everything else for the better.

There's a type of tenacity that comes from tuning in to this side of you, where the sense of purpose and meaning reaches far beyond yourself. On some level, our souls are all connected, and contributing to the whole in some way will solve a sense of separation that you feel between yourself and the wider world. As with everything I've written about so far in this book, the things we'll feel intuitively called to protest against will be different from person to person.

There are still wars going on in the world, so you may feel it's your job to put an end to one through the legal structures and systems of diplomacy that are already in place. It could be that you feel it's most urgent to stop the depletion of natural resources, and so you want people to have more awareness about the environmental impact of the products they're buying, such as ones containing palm oil. You might want to campaign for something in your local area to benefit your home town. You could start a petition or organize a march. You might find that you need to fight through your own beliefs, stories and things that are holding you back in your own mind. You'll most likely need to fight through other people's opinions of what you should or shouldn't be doing, but you can act in spite of all these if you know what change you're being called to create.

The cause that's calling you

Real and seismic change can result from a collective desire to make momentum, and if there's a movement we feel inspired by and passionate about, we can initiate a shift in opinion in whichever direction we feel called. The #BlackLivesMatter and #MeToo movements were prime examples of this. The BLM movement grew as a global conversation about how to create lasting change in order to correct an imbalance of power that had caused voices to be suppressed and lives to be lost due to racial injustice. People everywhere shared stories, messages and content to contribute to the movement in their own way – whether it was petitions, protests or posts online. The urgent need for change was palpable, and by harnessing collective power through a tool that we all have at our fingertips, the movement took society to a new level of awareness regarding race.

Another online movement that raised awareness and created a change in attitudes was the #MeToo movement. It would probably have been safer and easier for the women who added their voices to the #MeToo movement to have never said anything, shown their support or shared their stories of what happened to them. Some of them were hugely successful actors with reputations and future jobs at risk, but they spoke up anyway because they were telling the truth of what had happened to them. They knew that by doing so they'd inspire other women to do the same, while also letting others know that they weren't alone in their trauma. Any fear of speaking out was overtaken by a strong need to fight for something, and a belief that it was more important to do that first and then overcome any obstacles that might arise from the decision to speak out.

There are certain causes that millions of us are passionate about and feel called to protest for (such as racial equity and addressing the climate crisis), but there are also causes that will be smaller and feel more personal to you. This could be something happening in your local area, or something in your child's school that you know needs to be improved. It could be an urge to teach on a topic that could help other survivors who have gone through a trauma similar to something you've experienced yourself. Or it could be leading the way to change as part of a charity or organization that's already taking action.

Finding a cause to be passionate about is the key, because when you tune in to that deep desire to keep pushing for change, you'll find yourself being fuelled by a source of energy that exists outside your own internal motivations. You may also find a sense of purpose here when you're signing petitions, volunteering for organizations doing good in the world or just setting up a monthly donation to a charity that you think is doing amazing work, even if it's only a small amount. Whatever a meaningful contribution looks like for you, there will always be causes calling you to harness your power for a greater good.

If you're still trying to figure out which cause has the most meaning for you, a big clue to understanding what you actually do believe in can be knowing what you absolutely don't believe in. Those things that are so repulsive to you that you can't bear to live in the same world as them are the things you'll fight to live without. Think of the last time you felt so frustrated and enraged that you had to turn off the television; or when you needed to close the newspaper mid-article because you couldn't bring yourself to read any more; or when something you saw stuck with you for so long afterwards that you wish you'd done something differently to prevent it. These moments from the past that gave you a strong sense something was wrong could be the signs pointing you towards your future.

Intuition in action: feelings in the body (bad)

Our intuition will often be experienced in our body because it's the most obvious way for us to feel things. While intuition in our mind so often gets ignored, when it strikes us in a physical way we're much more likely to pay attention, such as when we get a bad feeling, which we can interpret as a signal that there's something to move away from, change or delete from our life.

This may manifest as a knot in your stomach, a sinking feeling in your gut, a full-body flare up of resistance, or sometimes a feeling of literal nausea and sickness. When this happens as a reaction response, it's a sign that something isn't sitting well with you. If you're consistently facing something that's out of tune for you, such as returning every day to a job that's no longer serving you, it can flood your body with dread, raising your cortisol levels and eventually leading to anxiety and nightmares.

Why does this happen? Evolution. Our ancestors needed to intuit when something in the vicinity wasn't in their highest good so that they knew to move away before being killed – for example, by a snake or tiger lurking in a nearby bush. Our intuition is something that has deteriorated with our evolution rather than improved, as we've become conditioned to always be distracted and ignore our unexplained senses. Intuition is a vital tool that supports us to stay well and keeps us in situations that serve us best, so noticing the negative signals your body sends you can connect you with the innate intuitive awareness of your ancestors.

Modern-day threats are different, of course, but our body can still tell us what we need to move away from. When you see an injustice, it'll still trigger a fight-or-flight response, and this can be a sign from your intuition calling you to take action against it. Anger, rage, disgust and dismay are responses telling you that there's a chance for something to be better if you can figure out how to improve it. Notice when your body says 'no' to something and how it expresses this for you in your own unique way, as when you start fully feeling into the dis-ease and dis-comfort, you'll have a clear, undeniable sense of what you need to change.

Be a catalyst to create change

Being deeply affected by something is a catalyst for change, and by knowing what you feel is wrong, you'll find your justification for fighting for what's right. You can't ignore the harrowing feelings that move you and affect you, and you're not meant to. So, imagine how fulfilling it would be if you could spend the rest of your life creating lasting change and moving the mountains that haven't yet been moved? By fighting the good fight, you could create more moments worth remembering and see less of the things that you'd rather forget. Undoubtedly, those same things that move you, repulse you and compel you will do the same for others too and, with the tools we have access to today, it won't take long to create a community (or join an existing one) of those fighting for the same cause as you.

By doing good in the outer world because you have an inner desire to do so, you're aligning with the impact you're really here to make. You're not meant to be passive in your own life or in the lives of others if you know how to make them better. You're not supposed to keep looking down at your feet if you can see the way forwards. When a new movement beckons, lead the way for people if it's what your intuition is telling you to do in order to create the change your soul wants to see. You might just be the one who'll whip away a dusty old cloak of darkness to reveal the light that was always hiding underneath. If the future depends on what you do in the present, what can you start fighting for now to create the type of future you'd want to be a part of? Inside everyone is one cause that hits deeper than the rest, and noticing what this is will be an indicator of what your intuition is urging you towards.

We all have our own ways of fighting for what we believe in and it doesn't necessarily have to look like protesting on the street, but next time you do see people protesting, notice their faces and put yourself in their shoes. They might look peaceful and determined, or angry and enraged, but behind that is a strong belief in a better world they can envision in their minds. Otherwise, they wouldn't bother protesting. They're hoping to achieve an outcome that they *know* is possible and they're willing to do something about it. This force is also what brings people together, and then bonds them together, through a shared effort and experience.

Whatever personality traits you think you have – humble, quiet, bold or brave – you have enough to elevate the importance of an issue you care about. All you need to do is find your own way to make the world listen to what you have to say. When you find what you want to speak up for, you can make the world your microphone until everybody listens. Being committed to a cause is what gives us purpose, and by helping others to thrive in some way we give ourselves a reason to keep moving every day. When there's a war for you to win, it doesn't need to be won with anger, force or might – you can be just as strong on a chariot of light.

Journalling questions to go deeper into Protest

/ What injustice upsets you the most?

/ How can you create a community around what you want to change?

/ What is it important that people listen to you about?

Pursuit

Question 7: What are you always seeking?

....

'We are what we repeatedly do.'

Will Durant

The common thread between all the things you've done before and will do in the future is a quest to find what you're always seeking. When you know what that is, you can align your life with a smoother journey and find fewer of the pitfalls that inevitably show up if you're busy chasing the wrong thing. To find out what you're really seeking, you need to get really, *really* honest with yourself. Your intuition will tell you when something isn't going to give you the result you want from it, but it's not always the easiest thing to hear and accept. Receiving what you want in the quickest timeframe possible means going after it – only it and nothing else – while keeping your intentions clear and free from distractions.

What you pursue is decided by you

As much as our intentions can become skewed by other people's expectations and by society's ideas of where we should be and by when, only we can ultimately decide our fate. Our destiny is for us to reach, and we get to choose what we pursue. A lifetime spent pursuing something other than the things we really want will still be full of lessons and experiences, but we might be left feeling like we never quite got to where we wanted to go. So, how can you find out what you're always seeking? With the most accurate and intelligent assessment tool that you have at your disposal: your intuition.

Once you realize that you're always seeking something, you can shift timelines and cross over into new realities, where you'll meet less resistance because you're on your highest path. The chase is a lot more fun and a lot more fulfilling when it's fuelled by purpose and meaning, and when it's heading to a destination that you're sure on a soul level you want to go to. Recognizing in yourself the symptoms of being out of tune is almost always a result of following a route other than the path your intuition is trying to lead you down. Uncovering the 'shoulds', 'buts' and 'ifs' underneath every decision you make will show you where you've been taking yourself off-track as a result of being led by something other than your own dreams and inner direction.

What you're pursuing will show up consistently through how you act and the way you spend your time. For example, you may find that you're always being a counsellor to your friends and family because you're pursuing your goal of everyone being as happy and secure in themselves as they possibly can be. You may find that you spend your mornings writing in your journal and that when you do, beautiful passages emerge that you realize are meant to be shared with more people than just you in the privacy of your bedroom.

You may find that you move between jobs and offices always feeling trapped and never able to be your individual self – in which case, perhaps your soul is suited to being an entrepreneur. These were all signs for me, showing me that the way I spent my time was telling me to be a spiritual coach, author and entrepreneur.

Knowing and recognizing these patterns within yourself is how you can reclaim power in your life and stop spending time on things that aren't going to pay off with a sense of satisfaction and purpose. Giving your power away to allow other people to decide what you're meant to be seeking in life is a lesson that hopefully you'll only need to learn once; although, if you fail to notice it and don't make a drastic change in how you live your life, you can feel the pain of being out of tune over and over again. If you know where you want to go, the way to stay on track is to keep asking yourself why you're doing each thing that you're doing, and if it's really going to help you to reach the best possible version of your life any faster.

This process will reveal any fears and insecurities that are guiding your decision-making. It will help you to see when being scared is taking priority over surrendering to being fully soul-led. You can direct yourself onto any path in life that you want to be on, and this gets a whole lot easier to do when you know *why* you want to reach a certain destination.

Why? Why? Why?

The 'why?' method is something I use with my coaching clients because it helps them to get to the root of what their underlying motivations are. The things pushing us forwards can be coming from an inspired and aligned place – or, perhaps more often, from triggers and wounds we're acting out of and trying to cover up by getting a certain end result.

Using the 'why?' method will help you establish which of the above applies for you when you have a decision to make or you're finding yourself constantly hitting walls because nothing seems to be working. The first step is to give yourself a stern, hard talking-to and ask yourself with total, brutal, unflinching honesty why you're actually doing something. Then, when you've got that answer, ask yourself again: *why* do you want that? And then, again: why do you want *that*?

I usually find that three 'whys' are sufficient, but you can keep going for as long as you feel necessary, watching out for any feelings which may hint that your intuition is telling you there's still another layer to uncover here. If you can't completely settle in to the answer and feel that it's 100 per cent truth for you on a soul level, then you probably haven't got to your deepest 'why'.

We often talk about our 'why' with respect to our purpose – the reason we're on Earth and our mission while we're here – and using this method can also give you a clue to your deepest 'why'. For example, when I'm working with people who have a spiritual business and are feeling confused because they have so many different services they want to offer, I'll ask them to condense the impact they want to make down into one statement. This one statement about how they can provide a transformation for someone ultimately reveals their main 'why' – what they're really trying to achieve while helping clients using their different skills and offerings.

You can use this method when you're in a relationship crisis and trying to understand why something doesn't feel quite right for you anymore, just as you can use it when you're trying to decide whether or not to spend a lot of money on a house move. I'm sure you've had situations before when you've made decisions from a place that you realized wasn't coming from inside of you and then felt utterly disillusioned with the outcome, losing interest in it quickly and blaming yourself for not listening to your intuition sooner.

This can happen when we're in a rush, we're under pressure or we're simply just not listening. To avoid the external pressures and expectations that might drown out the quiet but clear inner knowing of why you really want to be here, take yourself out of the rat race for a moment and commit to yourself that you're going to understand your biggest motivations.

Intuition in action: getting away from it all

Pulling over from the mental traffic of everyday life will allow you to tune in and get clear, unhindered clarity on what's directing you and driving you. As someone who's been trapped in the rat race for many years in different guises, I know how addictive it can be, but I promise you: there are huge insights to be gained if you're willing to step out of your regular routine and spend some time alone.

I know it's not easy for everyone to do this, with a job, kids, houses to clean, people to care for and money to be made; but once in a while, however you can, please do take time out to get back in tune with yourself. Having alone time is a luxury and a privilege because it enables you to see yourself in a way that's not influenced by other people's opinions. When you're on your own, you don't have to present as anything or be anyone that you're not.

So, for this exercise, I want you to commit to one break from your life, by the end of this book, when you spend time alone. Then, make it a regular practice (in a way that works for you) to get some time on your own so you can pause and reflect on whether you really feel in tune with what you're doing and where you're going. You can feel into things so much better when you're not influenced by others, especially if you're a sensitive person who's extremely empathic. Our own boundaries and beliefs can become so blurred when we're always trying to serve everyone else, which can cause us to pursue things that aren't in our own best interest because we're more focused on other people than ourselves.

One way to take time out and reflect is by going for a walk in nature. Dogs are said to be man's best friend and maybe it's because they give you a chance to take a break with just you and your four-legged friend, who probably won't have much to say. For me it's always a solo walk by the sea, because I'd learned by my late 20s that I'm living my best life when I'm at the coast, but for you it might be in a local park, by a pond or through a nearby field or forest. Getting into nature is one of the best ways to feel awe and connection, and to ground yourself into the natural world, which we're all still an intrinsic part of.

Just the mental space that a break provides could be exactly what you need to have a breakthrough. What was Isaac Newton doing when he discovered gravity? Sitting under a tree watching the world go by. What did Buddha spend his time doing between coming out with profound lessons and teachings? Meditating, also under a tree... How many times have you come back from holiday with a whole new perspective on the fact that your love life needs a boost, your home town needs to change or you're in totally the wrong career?

These insights will fall into your head when you're not thinking about anything else, so try to take a rest as often as possible. In solitude, you can receive answers as to what you really want from life. Schedule regular breaks into your diary and you'll find that, in the space you make, you recover parts of yourself that have been hidden by the hustle, bustle and distractions of everyday life.

It's never enough if it's the wrong thing

You can always use the technique of figuring out what *isn't* 'it' to find out what is. When the pursuit of something ends badly, it could be because you realized that what you were pursuing wasn't what you wanted at all. Or it could be that you were on the right path but there was a lesson to learn to help you do better next time. There will be a very distinct difference between how you feel in these two scenarios: in one instance, you'll want to pick yourself up and keep trying; whereas in the other, you'll want to kick yourself for not recognizing what you were doing wrong sooner.

An achievement doesn't feel like an achievement on the inside if we don't know the purpose of it and if it's not getting us any closer to where we really want to be. The mirages that we spend a long time struggling to reach can instantly evaporate the second we arrive, leaving us not knowing what else to do but start chasing the next one, hoping to find something different. This isn't to say that having a strong drive to achieve goals is a bad thing; it's definitely not – in fact, it's a key part of building resilience and creating success. However, if you're always running, yet never feeling any more satisfied, then it's a symptom of being out of tune.

As I've described earlier, when we're not listening to our intuition, it may take physical things to make us notice – either in our body or from the way the world is showing up to us. Meeting block after block is often a sign of a block within ourselves, when we're going after the wrong thing, which is never going to give us what we really need in order to flourish, grow and express as our soul self. Whether it's something spiritual or something physical, what we're seeking is out there somewhere in some realm or dimension, and if we meet it in ourselves first, we'll find that the journey towards what we're trying to get to will be so much easier.

We're a magnet for the things that we most want to meet, so it's vital we understand what we really want to attract. Once we do, we're able to pursue things that will immediately help us prosper rather than revealing what we still have to learn about ourselves. By taking time for yourself and escaping the noise, you might find that the answers to what you're always seeking have been showing themselves to you all along – through every action you've taken, every experience you've had and every lesson that you've learned.

The deepest desire beneath it all could be a soul longing to spend time with yourself instead of being someone for everyone else, and to be the best version of you by leaving behind anything that doesn't feel aligned. You're not meant to be a puppet for other people's desires; unless you were born with marionette strings, you're here to pursue the unique soul essence of you and nothing else. If you feel like you're always seeking and never finding, then there's more to uncover about the real you. That's the ultimate destination you're trying to reach: trying to see yourself at a soul level so that you can rest into who you really are. That squirming feeling that something isn't right, which makes you keep moving, can be a signal that you're looking for something to cure the itch.

When we get to know what we're always wanting, we can tune out of anything that isn't it. The internal driving force that urges us forwards can be a huge positive momentum for change if we're facing in the right direction. To make our hearts as full as our calendars, we need to make sure that we're aware of and deeply connected to what we're really in pursuit of.

Journalling questions to go deeper into Pursuit

✏ If money didn't exist, how would you want to spend your time?

✏ If you could achieve one thing by the end of your life, what would it be?

✏ What's the best way for you to use your energy?

Possibilities

Question 8: What's the greatest thing that could be possible for you?

....

'I AM the greatest. I said that even before I knew I was.'

Muhammad Ali

Seeing the truth of who you are means asking your mind to think more of you by believing in the best being possible. The sky is only off-limits if you decide it is, and nothing can hold you back more than you and the decisions you make. By deciding to accept that your destiny is to live the greatest possible version of reality, you'll start seeing the ways in which what you want can become available to you. Your intuition is capable of showing you how you can expand far beyond your current reality, so to fully accept and follow what it says will require you to leave your limits behind.

Bigger vision, better results

When you stretch your vision, you make room for your desires. Keeping your ideas small and limited is like keeping your vision in black and white – missing out on all of the excitement and bold, vivid colour that's readily available for you to access if only you'd tune in to a different channel. As a human with many different options in front of you as to which path you could walk and which timeline you could be on, you're fully entitled to choose the best possible one for you.

It seems obvious when it's written down as words on paper, yet why do we sometimes not do this and end up out of tune instead? We live within the limits of our beliefs, and if we look at those who have achieved exceptional things within their lifetime, there's always a common theme: they had a firm belief that each goal they were pursuing was within the realm of possibility for them. The earlier we decide something isn't possible, the sooner that potential future outcome disappears in front of us. Believing in exceptional outcomes also means having an exceptional level of belief in our own potential to get us there, which is something we can choose to tune in to. Our intuition is limitless and so are we; and to remind ourselves of this, it can be helpful to have expanders.

Expanders are those people you've never met who can inspire you to accept only the best for yourself. Your expander is simply a person you've chosen because something in their story resonates with you and you admire the results they've achieved – but remember that they're just human too! Some people are born rich and go on to get richer. Some people have famous parents and go on to be famous themselves. But there are also people who grow up poor, with everything against them, and go on to break records and become world-famous for their talents.

Choosing the script of someone you like the look of can remind you of what's possible if you rewrite your own story. For example, I find Eminem's story to be a massive inspiration. He grew up in a rough neighbourhood in Detroit and was so violently bullied at school that he once had to spend five days in hospital with a cerebral haemorrhage. He began pursuing his rap career as a teenager and continued chasing it for years, even after being evicted and locked out of his home, forcing him to break a window to sleep on the floor with no heat, water or electricity.[3] Now, he's one of the most successful rappers and musicians of all time.

Again, this isn't to say that you should be idolizing anyone, but rather that you should see your shared humanity and on that basis view yourselves on an equal level, so that it reinforces your belief in the possibility of achieving your goals in this lifetime. It's also important to remember that these people aren't superhuman and they're not completely free of limiting beliefs. They will have had doubts, bad days and things they regret from their past. The only difference is that they did *the thing* anyway.

One of my favourite quotes ever is by Henry Ford, who said, 'Whether you believe you can do a thing or not, you are right.' As soon as we think we can't, we cut off that option and are left with a lesser alternative. Our limiting beliefs are like layers keeping the sky above us cloudy and stopping us from seeing the stars, so when we see them for what they are and try to move past them, we enter the endless space of the unknown, where we can see what's possible beyond the world we're currently living in.

Are you lying to yourself with a limited vision?

Often our limiting beliefs hold us back without us even realizing they're there. To figure out what yours are, you can make a list that will show you on paper how and why all of your limiting beliefs are actually lies. When I'm working with a client who feels stuck under their limiting beliefs, I'll ask them to voice-note me every single time a limiting belief comes up, and you can do this for yourself with a pen and paper or the voice-note memo app. The reason for doing this is to show you how many limiting beliefs you have and to help you recognize what they are in the moment when they come up.

Recognizing them and exposing them is like bringing a shadow out in front of you into the light – it's so much harder for it to exist when it's not being hidden behind your back, where you can't see it. Doing this exercise on a regular basis definitely requires huge commitment to seeing your ceilings and learning your limits, but just noticing and listing those limiting beliefs you have will allow you to act consciously against each one until, ultimately, you're able to dismantle them completely because they have no basis for surviving in your subconscious anymore. For example, you might have limiting beliefs around getting yourself up earlier to start that exercise routine or write that book you've always wanted to write, because you believe it just isn't possible for you to change your routine. Write it down and ask yourself why you think that is, and if it's really true. Then ask yourself: what can you do to overcome it and prove that it's a lie?

You might have a limiting belief that you're too shy to speak to an audience online or lead an in-person class or workshop. Why do you think this is? Where did it come from, and how can you prove it wrong? The same could apply for a limiting belief you might have around money or anything else that's restricting your outlook on the possibilities available to you. Note: limiting beliefs often have no foundation whatsoever in what's actually possible for your reality.

Keeping your vision smaller than you are is an uncomfortable lie to be living in because you'll always feel as though something is 'off' and out of tune. The feeling of wasted potential is something that definitely isn't in line with your highest self, so keeping your view of the options available to you as wide as possible will help you to get closer to the truth of what you want. If you don't accept what you really want, you'll never take the steps to get there and might invest all your time in a smaller vision that's never going to feel 100 per cent right. When you know you're meant for more, it's because you are, and your inner self is giving you a sense of the possibilities that are within reach for you in this lifetime.

A big sign of being out of tune in this way is if, when you see people living an amazing life with a great relationship, loads of money and/or success in the field that you want to be in, you feel intense bitterness, jealousy and resentment. When you find yourself feeling annoyed and bitching to your friends about these people, it's because you really want what they have but due to your own limiting beliefs you're denying yourself the chance to actually go for it. By contrast, when you tune in to that vision of what's possible and accept that you want it, you'll instead feel inspired by successful people. You'll start looking for clues in what they've done and use them as a model for your success. Seeing those who already have what you want can actually serve and help you, by getting you closer to it instead of denying their joy and denying the truth about the life you really want to be living.

I have found that the things you sense you want most on a soul level can quickly become part of your life if you accept that you *do* really want them. This is because our intuition is pointing us towards the things that are meant for us through our desires. If you're lying to yourself by keeping a vision that's smaller than your potential in this lifetime, then you'll always feel like a little bit less than you're worth. To get past this means you need to keep your vision big and review it often, to see where it can be bigger, better and more in tune with the real you.

Intuition in action: virtual vision board

Gone are the days of a paper vision board – if you want to save on ink, do it online instead. That said, if you're someone who prefers their possibilities to be shown to them in paper form, you simply need to look online or in magazines to find pictures of the people, places and possibilities that inspire you the most. Print or tear them out, mixing it up with pictures and words, and make sure you connect with every image or phrase on there. For example, you could cut out little pictures of your own face and stick them over those of the people in the scenes on your vision board. (I've been known to put a photo of my head on the front of *Vogue* and *TIME* magazine covers!) Then, keep it on your wall, or somewhere you can look at it every day, so that your subconscious can see that it's totally normal for these things to be around you in your present reality.

If you want to opt for the online version, sign up for a free Pinterest account and create your first 'board'. You then simply search for the word you want and 'pin' the pictures you like to your virtual vision board. This is the method I recommend because you can update it and add or remove pins as your vision changes. However, even when what you want starts arriving, leaving the things you've already created on there will only help you to believe that it's *all* possible, because you've got some of it already. Take a screenshot of your Pinterest vision board and make it your laptop background and/or phone screensaver. The more you assimilate the images into your mind, the more you get used to them and the more you believe they're possible. You don't want your desires to stay separate from you, so the way to close that gap is by making them a normal part of your reality.

Even better than expected...

The possibilities available to you may be even bigger than you can possibly anticipate. This is why so many people live by the phrase 'this or something better'. How many times have you had a situation not turn out how you thought it would, but at the end of it all you were incredibly grateful because it worked out so much better? Leaving a little room for the Universe to add its magic touch works wonders for your dreams and future. 'This or something better' leaves space for the outcomes and potentialities that are beyond even the biggest vision you can comprehend right now. Things work out in more imaginative ways all the time, and with hindsight, it's often the only way we can recognize miracles for what they really are.

Being soul-led means surrendering to the fact that you don't know it all and you're not meant to, because there's an interweaving force connecting all things together, including you within it. Your best outcomes of all may be ones you couldn't imagine, even when you're being brave in the face of your limiting beliefs and making rules for reality that reach way beyond what's expected of you. What you want for your life may change, and if so, your intuition will tell you that immediately. You may be so sure that you want something for weeks, months or even years, until one day the thought of it makes your stomach drop – like there's something massively wrong with the vision now because it doesn't fit you anymore.

As much as you can allow your intuition to lead you to the best things possible, you can also allow it to lead you away from the things that once seemed great but don't anymore. Let go of any illusions about what's impossible for you and let your intuition lead you to the best possible life you deserve. You get to let your life be an example to yourself and others to show what you're capable of, and your desires are the directions to what will feel most in tune for you in that moment. When you notice potential outcomes that inspire you, that's your intuition giving you a green light to accept it as yours and start moving towards it.

If an idea feels really good to you then it's good to go for it and see what happens. You won't be led down paths where there's nothing for you to learn when you're living in tune with your intuition and guided by your gut feelings, trusting yourself more than anything else. Your own guidance is the glue holding your future vision together. So, accept the vision as already yours. Don't let the limits lead you to believing that less is available to you than it actually is – there's a whole world of possibility and opportunity available, and if someone else has had it, then so can you.

You don't have to live under any lies your limiting beliefs tell you. They were made by you, so you also have the power to remove them by confronting them and proving what they are: lies that keep your future limited. When you think your vision is big, go bigger and then bigger. Be prepared for the Universe to one-up your plans and make them even better than you were imagining. Let your intuition lead the way while trusting that your own desires are the most important direction that you need to tell you what's next and what could really happen for you. You can only find out what you're capable of if you try for the best outcome possible.

Journalling questions to go deeper into Possibilities

✎ What is your biggest, boldest desire?

✎ How are you limiting your vision of the future?

✎ If great was guaranteed, what would you choose?

Purge

Question 9: What ideas do you need to let go of?

....

'Waking up to who you are requires letting go of who you imagine yourself to be.'

Alan Watts

While knowing what you do want, it's just as important to be very clear about what you don't want. All of our individual beliefs meet and mesh together, creating a whole mental system that forms our idea of what life can or can't be for us. This means that we go into things based on a viewpoint we've adopted over time, which might be separate from our soul-aligned desires. Being influenced by things other than our intuition will happen more often if we don't regularly review and cut loose from any mental or emotional ties that are holding us back from tuning in effectively. Finding your most purposeful life will require untangling your own dreams from other people's ideas of what you're meant to be doing, so that you can live fully in line with what you've decided is possible for you.

Moving the milestones

One thing that will really get in the way of your intuitive sense is taking on other people's ideas of where you should be and when, making you worry that you're doing something wrong, even if the path you're on is actually much more in tune for you. How many times have you felt pressure to be at a certain point in your life by a certain time, and then felt like you fell short because you didn't make it there? Or maybe you did get there, and then you realized that it actually wasn't what you wanted at all?

We're often told that we 'should' own a house, stay in one job for our whole lives and accept the norms that other people have accepted. In a corporate job, we're told that we 'should' climb the ranks, just be happy with four weeks' holiday a year and put in extra hours if we want to succeed. Moving towards milestones that we never really wanted to meet can feel hugely overwhelming, and anxiety is an insidious enemy of intuition.

Once you arrive at these milestones, you might feel as though you've achieved something but that it's not quite as good as you thought it would be. It's a shame to find that something is out of tune for you after you've spent a long time working to get there, so to figure out whether you really want to meet certain markers because they're truly aligned with your soul, you need to know the difference between being guided by your thoughts or by your feelings.

Knowing this distinction can save you from making decisions based on your ideas of what life 'should' be, rather than what you truly want it to be. Your ideas of who you are and who you 'should' be might be very different, and to tell the difference between the two will require you to know whether you're thinking something or feeling it. Staying in our head keeps us in our mental thoughts and programming, instead of our soul-centred intuition – which is usually felt and sensed, rather than tangled up within our internal monologue.

Intuition in action: thinking or feeling?

Telling the difference between these two ways of sifting through information is extremely challenging at first and requires a lot of patience and dedication to understanding yourself. Your mental programming is constantly trying to keep you thinking; the chatter in your brain is quick to over analyse and quick to question everything. Feeling your way into an idea may be slower to give you a response, but it'll be less likely to change once you reach your answer.

Our thoughts can be very fickle, switching and changing constantly between what we should or shouldn't do. When we're feeling into an idea with our intuition, we'll be quite sure of the answer – especially once we get used to trusting it and prove to ourselves that it always leads us to the best outcome. This is when we can really let go of old ideas and mental programming to trust our intuition more than anything else: once we've found out the benefits for ourselves a few times and know that we can immediately trust our intuitive instincts over our mental thoughts – even when it feels like a massive leap and we have no idea of the outcome.

Your intuitive feelings can often go completely against your logical thoughts, which is why it can be so hard to trust them. But, again, have you had a situation before when you've gone with a thought over a feeling and then regretted it? Remember this and try differently next time. Having enough evidence is what will solidify your trust in your feelings, rather than succumbing to your thoughts, which may be skewed by ideas and belief systems that you've taken on in this lifetime.

To practise this, start with something small. When you have a daily decision to make that doesn't have much consequence, sit with it for a second and see:

✦ How do you feel about it?

✦ What do you think about it?

✦ Are these two things the same or are they different?

When you find that there's a mismatch, practise taking a leap and going with your feeling first, even when it doesn't make logical sense. By testing the waters with these smaller decisions, you'll hopefully build your sense of trust. Realizing that you're always led to the right answers when you follow your feelings over your thoughts will prove to you that it's safe for you to follow your intuition, even when your feelings about which direction to go are unexplained by your logical reasoning.

By feeling into everything we've taken on as truth, we can untangle our thoughts from our individual inner knowing, taking us towards a more accurate sense of who we are and why we're really here. It's only by feeling what our honest truth is with the internal intuition that lives in our wise, unyielding gut that we can stay on our most purposeful path. Otherwise, it can seem simpler to follow the signposted road other people have taken – until we realize that it's not heading where we want to go at all. We're the only ones who can recognize our own individuality and feel what we *do* and *don't* want.

Once you tune in to recognizing what feels bad just as much as what feels good, you can start to steer your life away from things that don't suit you by noticing the red flags. Resistance is a red flag, and really recognizing these feelings when they come up is how you can choose to move back into alignment. Red flags are felt in the moments when you know that something isn't right – and more often than they're seen, they're felt. Even if you don't know what the better option is yet, or even if you don't think you deserve better, you know when something is wrong – and that's when it's not 100 per cent right.

Ideas of reality that aren't yours

For as long as I could remember, I'd dreamed of moving to California. Anywhere with more sun would do, but every time I went to California for a road trip with my lifelong bestie, it felt more like home to me than anywhere else I'd ever been. When I got back to England, I'd always be California daydreaming and watching television programmes about people who'd given up everything to opt for simpler lives, either in the wild or in tiny homes. With not much more than a few practical things like pots and pans, they were able to do more of what they loved and less of what they didn't because they had less *stuff* to worry about and pay for. They'd all tried the regular route and felt deeply that it wasn't meant for them, with most of them sharing the same life story of finding themselves in an office cubicle every day to sustain an out of tune life they'd fallen into.

This kind of nomadic lifestyle they'd opted for isn't for everyone and it wasn't for me either – but there was still something I could see in the lives of these people that intuitively felt appealing. They felt free, they were living life on their own terms, and they were able to travel to some of the most exotic and untouched corners of the world. Like so many people today, I felt like I was missing all of these things despite having so many *things*. When you're out of alignment with what you really want, the small feeling that something is missing always comes creeping back in. And for my husband, Ally, and I, the feeling was that a regular life wasn't really what we wanted. We wanted more money than just enough to survive on each month, less stuff, fewer obligations and commitments, and a lot more travel.

To be able to make all of this our reality would be anything other than quick and easy. We couldn't just down tools and hop on the next flight to somewhere sunny. It would require untethering ourselves from everything that we'd tied ourselves to, one by one. I didn't know how or if I'd ever be able to move to California, but the thought of the stars aligning one day so that I could and having to say, 'No, sorry – I've got too much to sort out here' was enough to make me realize that something absolutely had to change.

Finding out what you don't want can come out of left field in the most unexpected way with a sudden shift or tragedy that makes you question everything, but more often, it slowly comes to the boil after simmering under the surface of your subconscious mind. The only way to avoid reaching boiling point is to tune in to the most subtle of feelings that something is off. Everything that you agree to have in your life is a contract, so it's time to review absolutely everything you've signed a contract with. Which mental and emotional contracts do you intuitively feel that you want to uphold, and which ones do you want to cut? Every item in your home, every friend that you keep, every project that you're investing your time in is a contract you're deciding to keep yourself tied to.

The things that have a hold on us are often illusions – that we should be a certain way, think a certain way or want certain things. Is the idea that has a hold on you a belief that you must be a certain way to feel like you're a success to your mother or father? Is the idea that has a hold on you an unwillingness to lower your income temporarily, and therefore you're staying stuck in a job you hate? Or is the idea that has a hold on you a lack of love and faith in yourself that you can actually get and keep all the things you really want?

It's the 'shoulds' that get a hold on us, wrapping us in invisible binds that become harder and harder to find our way out of. They collect on top of each other, like layers of autumn leaves hiding the ground underneath and stopping it from seeing the sunlight. Being bound by the 'shoulds' makes us feel like we can't reach out for something different and makes us think that we need someone else to set us free and give us permission to be who we really are. It can be hard to notice them because although the things that have a hold on us may well be physical, more often they're mental. They're the identities, the constructs and the familiar beliefs that are rooted in our subconscious perception of what reality means.

Emotional baggage that isn't yours to carry

When we let that baggage go, we set ourselves free. We feel lighter. We have more mental, emotional and energetic space. And it's from this place of space and serenity that we can really start to hear our intuition. When we're so used to looking outside ourselves for answers, it can be shocking once we see the parts of our life that had never really been ours because we gave them away so easily. By deciding to reclaim your fate, you can fill your life with so many more of the things that you actually *do* want.

You don't have to negotiate your dreams and desires if they're what feels most aligned for you and if there's even a tiny part of you that thinks they're possible. Your mental and emotional patterns inevitably create your internal reality so it's your job to choose ones that fit you. Being influenced by others is normal, so it's definitely nothing to be ashamed of, but know that you can always expand beyond your old ideas. They're only invisible constructs that you can change at any moment.

For example, the need to please or prevent others being angry is one idea that can keep us out of tune, as can the need for a sense of control because we want everything to be 'perfect'. Any ideas we have around control and perfection are exactly that – ideas – and are unlikely to result in an easy life of flow and freedom. They can also be manifestations of emotional baggage taken on at some point in life because of not feeling 'enough' or wanting to be seen a certain way in the eyes of the parents. Some ideas may have been a coping mechanism for trauma or a chaotic upbringing. There are so many layers that we have as multidimensional humans with many experiences, and our intuition is underneath it all. It's so important to notice when we have this emotional baggage because it can be another intuition-inhibitor.

Old relationships you're holding on to can also be coming from an idea that you need to keep certain people in your life, even though you actually don't. If you've ever had a toxic ex-partner or a friend you felt worse after seeing, you'll know this feeling. Sometimes it can even be a family member that you need to cut contact with, which might be the most painful purge of all. Your relationships are energy exchanges and a huge commitment of time and emotions. The relationships you have in your life can all be uplifting, inspiring and secure, but if you have someone in your life and you feel like you're never really sure where you stand with them, that's not security. If you have someone in your life who constantly brings your mood down, that's not a bond that's making you feel uplifted. And if during your time with someone you feel like you have to mask your success and achievements, that's only going to stifle your inspiration.

Emotional baggage can include needing approval, validation and wanting to fit in to a group. We have to get rid of our own toxic behaviour patterns and ways of being that have held us back so we can adopt new belief systems and ideas that are conducive to the results we want to create. We can't be the same person we used to be if we want to have a totally different life to show for it. By being different and doing different, we get to *have* different. This means that we need to get rid of all the old things that are preventing us changing ourselves if we want to have something new and something better. This means that a purge is always required to get to the next level and feel more in tune with the person we really want to be.

Is it okay to be with someone you're not 100 per cent sure you want to be with? Do you want to spend your time and energy in a way that you're not 100 per cent invested in spending it? Have you ever regretted making a decision that you weren't 100 per cent behind at the time? That point when you realize that you've fallen off-track because you were chasing ideas that weren't actually in tune for you is a scary but sobering moment. Remember that your intuition is just the purest form of you, so by feeling into your choices and making them from an authentic place, you can live in integrity with your own desires. Removing out of tune things from your life is what will set you free from everything you don't want so that you have room ready when something better arrives.

Journalling questions to go deeper into Purge

🖎 What holds you back from getting what you want?

🖎 What in your life feels limiting rather than expansive?

🖎 How have you been influenced by others to be where you are today?

Possessions

Question 10: How do your surroundings affect your intuition?

....

'Where there is too much, something is missing.'

Leo Rosten

Your space is sacred because it's where you can express the soul-aligned version of you. Whether you have a room or a house, the space you surround yourself with can either aid or inhibit your intuition, depending on how it makes you feel and what you keep within it. You can let go of anything that's stopping you from living in tune, and material possessions are probably the easiest thing of all to do that with. Items that aren't in tune with you are just another distraction that could be keeping you from a sense of ease, flow and purpose. Think of space as surrender. If you're being kept out of tune because of the things that belong to you, then that's something you can change with a commitment to clear and declutter your space.

Make space for movement and miracles

By making space, you set a clear intention with the Universe for what you're calling in to fill it. By purging the things you no longer want, you're closing the door on the past and opening a new one to your future. As you let go of those things that no longer serve you, you give yourself room to grow; as though you're cutting off the old, dead branches so that new green shoots can emerge next spring. Often, the things that we're unwilling to sacrifice are the things that are keeping us stuck. Letting go is your way of letting the Universe know that you're ready for something better – and this doesn't necessarily mean that by letting go of one handbag, you'll get another one in exchange. It might mean that by getting rid of things, you'll feel more free and ready to move, or you'll be able to take a pay cut and choose a better career because you realize that you can survive on a lower monthly budget than you've done previously.

Making space means that you're serious about filling it with something more special. Whether that's more time, more peace or an upgraded level of living, it's only by moving things out that you can move new things in. Once you've noticed what is out of tune for you, every day you're still keeping it is a choice. To make your life feel more in tune with you, create a plan to eliminate anything that's stopping you from feeling light, free and like the person you're meant to be.

Once you have fewer things to see through, you can see more clearly what you want to keep and what you do or don't really need. It also means that you can spend less time cleaning, tidying and sorting things out – and more time equals more room to be alone and do all of the exercises in this book. If moving into a more in tune life meant moving all of your belongings with you, would you be able to do it? You can always measure the items you have by this question.

Hoarding but not happy

On my own journey, it was when I started to realize what kind of lifestyle was really going to be in tune for me that I began to feel a deep discord with all the things I had around me. At one time in my life, I used to love collecting things and buying new outfits for nights out every weekend. I used to be a small-time hoarder because I hadn't yet looked far enough inwards to see that there was more my inner child needed than just things. The spiritual awakening process works in weird ways because you'd never think that it would lead to spending a year on Facebook Marketplace, listing things one by one. However, that's what happened to me. It wasn't because I was trying to become more Zen or thinking of moving to an ashram in India with nothing but a backpack and my Birkenstocks; it was just because I was connecting more with my inner self, and as that happened, my need for other things started to fall away.

I'd spent so many years trying to avoid this moment, fully buying into every excuse I was making that I didn't have enough time, was too tired from work and/or was hungover. Every space was filled and then some, including a spare, unsorted bedroom known as 'the junk room'. There were no nooks left and every cranny had been filled. The amount of stuff we were carrying weighed on more than just our home; we carried it at the back of our minds too. Decluttering was a big 'to-do' list item that we never wanted to do, so we never did. On top of this, our rooms at our parents' houses were still perfectly preserved time capsules of our former lives, almost untouched since we'd left for university with just a packed suitcase or two. As the years rolled on, our motivation dwindled, until the burden was enough to break our excuses. There was so much to get rid of, and it had got to the point where it was starting to hold us back.

I think this was around the same time that minimalism was taking hold as a huge trend, but that wasn't why I was doing it. I also wouldn't describe myself as a minimalist (and nor would anyone else who's seen my wardrobe) but I just knew that I had to make space for manifesting travel and be flexible enough to actually reach out and grab opportunities if they ever arose. Nothing was to go in landfill, so everything had to be sold, recycled or given away either for free or to a charity shop.

With every knock at the door, items started to slowly lift from our home. To say this process was tedious would be an understatement and it felt like it was never-ending. I didn't enjoy listing the things, and I certainly didn't enjoy all of the times when people didn't turn up to collect something and just chose never to reply to me again. However, the upside of doing it this way was that I managed to make quite a bit of money from all the items I'd sold.

Once our own house was clear, it was then time to move on to our childhood bedrooms. My home town was four hours away from where we were living, so I tackled it bit by bit. I found this process a lot more emotionally draining, because I was sorting through things from my childhood and teenage years, and going through more sentimental items like things that I'd put into a memory box – which itself was so overflowing that it barely stayed shut. For this reason, it was actually a blessing that I could only tackle it in small doses on my trips home, because I found that just going through each small piece of my past was so emotionally challenging that I actually couldn't face doing more in one go anyway.

Now that I've been through this process, I have a strict 'one-in, one-out' policy so that we never find ourselves in the same state again. As soon as I buy something to replace something else, the other thing gets sold straight away so that we never end up with any spare stuff. We don't have a loft or basement, or any other area full of clutter: just the things with a place in our home that we use and enjoy. The feeling of this is pure peace and I actually have a much better relationship with everything I own – and as a result, I don't feel the need to buy as much as I used to when I was blindly buying whatever I saw and liked. My decluttering journey taught me that getting rid of things from your life is one of the best ways to energetically up-level and align with what you want.

If you feel like you shouldn't get rid of things because you're lucky to have them compared to other people, then beware: making choices based on what you think other people's opinions are just keeps you feeling out of tune, because you're not making decisions based on what *you* actually want. Being radically honest about what you want means being radically honest about what you don't want either. Remember that it's not noble to do things that you don't want to do if you're not really being you.

Boundaries with buying

So much of what we buy is on impulse – especially if it's something small, cheap and inconsequential – but choosing things based on our intuition will lead to longer-lasting satisfaction with our purchase. Yep... you really can use your intuition for everything, and it will always lead you to the most satisfying results. Buying things isn't bad, but it's made a whole lot more fun and fulfilling when you're buying things that you really value and that are going to make your life better in some way. You can also use your intuition to put yourself in other people's shoes when you're buying a gift for them.

Empaths make great buyers for this reason! The more you bring your intuitive sense into shopping, the more you'll love your purchases and the happier you'll be with them for longer. When you're trying to decide whether a purchase you want to make is based on impulse or intuition, take a second to sense how the thing makes you feel. If your driver for buying is scarcity, that can seriously skew how accurately you assess whether you actually need it or not. I was an impulsive buyer for many years, so I know this feeling well. Unfortunately, I was also an impulsive buyer of tattoos, and they're a lot harder to get rid of! So, save yourself the regret and use this method instead...

Intuition in action: impulse or intuition?

It's important to figure out the difference between your intuition and an impulse because one will lead you to fulfilment, joy and alignment – and the other might lead you into a situation that you one day regret. If you're bullish and headstrong about chasing after something (I'm speaking to you, all of my fellow Taurus friends), then it may well be an impulse, because you don't have to be bullish about following your intuition – it's easy, it flows, it opens up an energetic path of opportunities. We feel the need to be gung-ho about following our impulses and knocking everything else out of the way to get them because those impulses are often coming from a place of fear and need.

If you have the feeling that you *need* whatever you're feeling an impulse for, or you simply *must* have something, then that's probably an impulse. An impulse is an unstoppable drive that's quick to arise, like an immediate longing. Intuition, on the other hand, is a knowing, a sensing or a gentle direction towards something. It can pop in faster than your first thought or it can reveal itself more slowly beneath the noise.

It thrives in the part of you where there's security, trust and peace. When you intuitively know something is right, you don't care so much about the timeline; maybe you've already noticed this when you've tuned into something that feels full of purpose. You know that it's going to be fulfilling, and you know that it's meant for you, so there's no need to rush. When you're following your intuition, things don't need to happen tomorrow.

You can ask yourself these questions:

✦ Do I need this *now*, or would I be happy to wait one/two/three/four years for the same outcome?

✦ Do I want it because I'm scared that if I don't have it now, I won't have it at all?

✦ Who am I without the thing that I'm urging for? Would I still be whole, complete and able to love myself?

You're controlled by your impulses, whereas you're called by your intuition. Next time you're feeling an internal nudge to go for something, and you're not sure which place it's coming from, consider why you want it and the emotions that it'd give you if you get it. If it's a short-lived high that you'll need another of, then it's an impulse. If it's something that will feel purposeful and aligned with the person you truly want to be, then it's your intuition.

....

When you go to buy something, check in first and see if it's actually going to improve your reality or if it's eventually going to make you feel more restricted. If you have multiples of the same item, then you can probably give it a miss. Every time you buy something, ask yourself if it's adding to what you've already got or if it's something you're going to regret buying in the future. Will it end up in a charity bag? Or will it be something that you're going to treasure and use for a very long time? Choosing what you're going to buy is an excellent exercise in tuning in to your intuition.

Possessions and objects aren't what fuel our purpose; they're distractions, more often than not. The life that inspires you is on the other side of all the things you're feeling weighed down by, which is why they might already feel slightly out of place in your reality. By letting them go, you let the Universe know that you're ready to receive something new that's meant for you. Release things if you feel that they're no longer serving you – otherwise they can drag you down and chain you to your old life so that you remain stuck, stagnant and unable to move forwards. It takes a lot of bravery to be willing to constantly update and renew the inventory of absolutely everything you're keeping in your life, but it's how you'll stay completely in tune with how you're living.

By knowing with certainty what you want to keep in your life and what you don't, you'll have more clarity on what you need to do to bring in the new. Through the space you make, you'll be able to see new possibilities and hear your heart more clearly when it's not being drowned out by everything that's dragging you down. To have something amazing that you really want, you need to say no to everything that isn't it. Let go of the bad to make way for the good. Let go of the old to make way for the new. Life is easier when it's only filled with the things that are meant for you.

Journalling questions to go deeper into Possessions

🖉 What belongings do you need to let go of?

🖉 How can you make space for the lifestyle you really want?

🖉 What have you been avoiding sorting through?

Panache

Question 11: When do you feel the most confident?

....

'As is our confidence,
so is our capacity.'

William Hazlitt

Knowing what you're great at will allow you to make a greater impact. When you can feel a spark within you that you have a special skill in something, that's your intuition telling you what you're being guided towards. Notice when you can *already* slip into ease, flow and joy, because when you've found what that is, you only need to focus on becoming even more skilled in it. It doesn't make sense to keep doing something that you have no confidence in, because there will be other options available that trigger less resistance in you. Do those instead, so you can use your time and energy in the best way possible. Your confidence in something is your calling towards it.

The path of least resistance

Once you start to realize when you feel the most confident, life will get easier and easier if you invest more of your time and energy there. I've learned that there are three ways to know what this is for you: resistance, reciprocity and recognition. Resistance is something that we all feel sometimes, and it's a feeling that hung over me all day, every day, for many years. For so much of my life, I was trying to force myself into a role that didn't fit me, and all along my body was screaming at me to stop. However, my mind was far too busy following what I thought I should be doing and trying to get certain outcomes rather than trying to tune in to a life that actually felt good.

Trying to live life this way created so much more stress, like I was trying to force a square peg into a round hole. If it doesn't fit, it doesn't fit – so why do we try and make ourselves into someone we're not? A lot of the time it's because we don't even notice the resistance. It can also happen because we're too busy following the 'shoulds' and the outcomes we want to get at the end, rather than our feelings. Or we can stay in a state of resistance because we feel trapped in a life that requires it. The practical reality is that it's not always going to be easy to move away from the path you've chosen previously and just switch quickly into something else, depending on what's going on in your life. But I do believe that it's possible for everyone to confidently move in a more aligned direction, with enough time to prepare and an open mind to see the opportunities that could make it possible.

Our intuition is calling us towards the things we find easy because that's the place we'll find we fit best. Whenever you feel resistance from now on – in your body, mind or emotions – know that it's your intuition telling you to tune in and ask why you're making things harder for yourself than they need to be. This can feel like a physical friction in your body, a mismatch between your internal world and the external life you're living, or a sense of dread that you feel every day.

On the other hand, you'll sense that there's no resistance when you're in flow with what feels easy because you're already feeling confident. Your soul wants you to choose the most natural way for you, and when that happens, life becomes easier because you're in tune. When you tune in with your intuition, it'll show you the easiest path, which we often say is the path of least resistance.

Notice where there's a positive value exchange

The path of least resistance will be illuminated to you through external signs – such as spooky synchronicities, repeating numbers and feathers falling in front of you – as well as through the things that light you up inside. This is the next piece, which is reciprocity. When you're confident about something, it'll create a positive value exchange that starts with how good it feels for you on the inside. I found that when I was following the path to a financial career, not only was I feeling so much resistance, but I also wasn't that good at it. I was okay, but I definitely wasn't great. I passed the maths module of my degree by only 5 per cent above a fail, and I also dreaded the seminars and lectures with a deep pit in my stomach because I didn't really understand what was going on.

The maths homework assignments were the ones I'd avoid at all costs, and I spent the day before my maths final exam with three girls I lived with in university halls, dying my hair. It's hilarious now to look back on that image of them all tugging at my head with tint brushes and bowl of bleach. I wouldn't have done it before other exams that I thought I had a shot at, but I knew the maths exam was going to be a disaster so I wasn't expecting anything other than to do badly. This is what I mean by reciprocity: when you think you're not good at something, you don't try as much and you don't do as well. However, when you feel that you have a certain skill at something, you'll put more effort into it and you'll get better results. This is another way that life flows so much more easily when you stick to what you feel confident doing.

The confidence will shine through as you explore your own capabilities. It will feel amazing, and when something naturally feels amazing it's your cue to keep doing it. This is as true in a physical, biological sense – eating feels good because you need to eat to stay alive – as it is in a spiritual, intuitive sense. The things that make you feel light and joyful are the things in this lifetime that will feel full of purpose for you, which is your intuition incentivizing you to keep doing them. Following the nudge within that you're really great at something will allow you to hone your skill at it, which will then build your confidence more and more. Recognizing this reciprocity and using it to your advantage is what will allow you to reach the pinnacle of whatever you're doing. When you give more of your true self, you'll get more positive things out of it in terms of the way you feel, the results you get and the impact you create.

What do you get noticed for?

Your confidence will show that you're clearly in tune with what you're doing, and people will start to recognize that and notice you. There's something intrinsic in your intuition that not only allows you to feel when you're gifted in something, but also allows you to feel the presence of other people's gifts. When you listen to a phenomenal speaker like Martin Luther King Jr., or hear the voice of an incredible singer like Whitney Houston, it makes you settle into a different space compared to when you're observing someone who's awkward or forcing themselves to do something they obviously don't wholeheartedly want to be doing.

This means that doing more of what you naturally feel confident doing will ensure people recognize you much more easily. If you find that you're getting frustrated by a lack of recognition or feeling like you're always overlooked, it could be a reflection of what you feel isn't really fitting within. Not only will our intuition make us feel resistance when we're out of tune, but the world will start showing it back to us too. To get more recognition, find what you're in tune with and confident doing, and eventually people will start to notice. Often when you listen to celebrity stories, you can hear how it only took one performance, after hundreds of others, for an important music executive to notice them, which was the big break into their A-list career. So, this isn't to say that recognition will come straight away, but when you have confidence in what you're doing, it allows you to keep going until you finally get that recognition, because all along you believed that you deserved it.

An example of this is Lady Gaga. To the world, it seems like she blew up overnight in 2008, but that one night of recognition, when Akon spotted her in a burlesque show, only happened after she'd performed hundreds of other shows in small New York bars. Once her talent had been spotted, more people started to recognize her and her fan base quickly grew around the world in response to her unique energy, voice and music style.[4] Now, everyone in the Western world knows who Lady Gaga is and the awards have followed. In her documentary (which is one of my favourites ever) she talks about how she can always find confidence again by grounding herself in her singing. When you're sure of what you're great at doing, you can always ground yourself in the thing that makes you feel the most confident, because it's a place where doubt doesn't exist.

You're naturally great at what you're meant to create

I was aware, when I was writing the journalling questions for this chapter, that they were going to bring up feelings of inadequacy for some people. That some people would read these questions and feel like they don't have anything they're good at, or be completely at a loss as to what they're meant to do because they don't feel like they can succeed in anything. If that's you, I want you to know and trust deep in your heart that neither of these things is true. Whatever it is for you, there's some skill within you that you can expand upon. If there's something that you love and you invest your energy into it, over time you'll improve and your confidence will build, until you get to a point when you can find an innate sense of worth in this work you're doing.

It could be writing, gaming, teaching, running, cooking, or caring for people or animals – but there will be something you can be confident doing, so by acknowledging what that is, you might start to realize that it's a piece of your purpose. Knowing your area of natural skill and the unique imprint that you can bring to it will unlock new levels of assuredness. The exact opposite happens when you're trying to push forwards with something you're out of tune with. If you're not sure yet what this thing is for you, start to notice when you feel more certain of your own ability and more confident about what you can create. Pay attention to what you find easy and what people ask you for help with. Bringing this to the top of your awareness will show you the clues that you may not have prioritized previously.

Client case study: spiritually shy to shining

When my client Sarah wanted to work with me, she had an Instagram handle and an idea of which way her intuition was pointing her towards: a soul-aligned career in spirituality. She was incredibly smart, funny and personable, and was making a six-figure salary in her full-time career in finance. We connected instantly over how similar our career stories were and how we both wanted to bring a new brand of grounded, practical spirituality into the mix. Sarah had begun her Human Design training, she had studied astrology for years and she felt a burning desire to start her own podcast. The only problem was that, so far, she'd been hiding in the spiritual closet from her friends and family – and now it was time to come out.

Sarah's story inspired me so much, and I wanted to include it here because she followed her calling towards the thing she knew was meant for her despite what other people would think – knowing that she'd have to face those close to her who had conflicting views about the messages she was sharing online. Day by day, she revealed more of her face, more of her voice and more of her personality online. It was easy for her to attract people to her content and paid readings because she was clearly so in tune with her topic and such a joy to work with. Being recognized for her skill and expertise, she was even asked to write about astrology for websites such as Bustle, Romper and Apartment Therapy.

As you read this chapter and start tuning in to what you know gives you confidence, remember that different situations will always arise where you'll need to prove to yourself how much you can show up for what you love. Your resilience and resourcefulness in response to controversy will repeatedly be tested as more people start to notice and recognize you, but stand firm in what you know makes you strong. You can do it well. You can excel. You can make a difference.

Confidence is calmness

It's the immense amount of confidence that comes from being in alignment that gives us the strength to overcome obstacles and climb to the top of whatever we're doing. The best athletes have confidence in how good they are because, without it, they wouldn't be willing to compete. When it comes to the things we think we're *not* good at, it's very unlikely that we'd commit enough to create any real success. Instead, we can choose to live more like Lady Gaga: finding confidence in what we love and grounding ourselves in it so that we can show it to the world regardless of what some people may think.

When we share our soul's strengths, eventually people will start to notice. It's that recognition that can lead us to endless wonderful opportunities and future successes. When we feel confident in how we're investing our time and energy, it gives us a sense of inner peace and satisfaction, and we're less likely to be shaken by the outside world or anyone else's opinions. When we value our feelings fully – like the answers to our prayers that they are – we become the ultimate authority on what we want, what we're meant to do and what our life is going to look like.

How you're being guided *to* or *away* from something will come through in how you feel. This includes the feeling of confidence and self-assurance that you're great at something. If you feel that way, it's probably because you are, and when you have that sense of confidence in what you're great at, you can show it off to the world with some serious panache. Your feelings are the divine neon signs that you have been looking for. When do you feel grounded and confident, calm and secure, and ready to take on the world?

Journalling questions to go deeper into Panache

🖊 When do you feel most secure in your ability?

🖊 What do people often invite you to do?

🖊 What do you have the potential to be really great at?

Passion

Question 12: What makes you feel the most excited and inspired?

....

*'In pleasant peace and security, how suddenly
the soul in a man begins to die.'*

Robinson Jeffers

It is possible to feel excited about everyday life. Not every day is going to be a whirlwind roller-coaster ride, and we probably wouldn't want it to be either (that would be exhausting). But when we do more of what we're excited about, inspiration flows more freely and our energy to keep going comes from inside of us, rather than from caffeine, energy drinks or any other artificial energy booster. Instead, inspiration can carry us through the day if we allow ourselves to follow what feels fun because we're on the path of least resistance.

Inspired action

Inspired action is inspiration in action. It's the first thing you lose when you're in a state of resistance, and it quickly dries up when you're pushing against the natural flow of who you are. This means that getting inspiration is a clue that you're on the best path for you. When ideas are flowing through easily and quickly – maybe so fast that you can't even keep up – then you've tuned in to something that is probably full of purpose for you. It's truly a magical phenomenon, like a river that opens up to you when you're just following the flow, with the next opportunity being lit up after the next, after the next...

Inspired action isn't just for artists or creatives; it's a way of committing to following your intuition by putting your own feelings and enjoyment of life first. You only get one time on Earth in this life, so how do you want to spend it? Do you want to be following the plan you've already made and doing what everyone else expects you to do? Or do you want to take each thing as it lights you up, unsure of where you're going next, but trusting in your own guidance to lead you to the best outcomes? Figuring out your action steps based on what lights you up is the 'secret sauce' talked about by many spiritual teachers.

Once inspiration takes over, it's all-consuming in the most wonderful way. What the clock says doesn't matter anymore. You might have to be pulled away from what you're doing, and you'll want to capture every sweet of drop of the endless inspiration as it flows through you and out of you. For me, the strongest connection with this feeling of passion is through writing – and on the days when I knew I'd be writing this book, I'd immediately wake up with a buzz as my brain came to and realized what was on the agenda for the day ahead. For some people, that passion may be found by serving others in a medical profession or by being able to see their children when they wake up. Like everything else in this book, it's totally individual and unique to you – but where you find inspiration is a clue for what you're most passionate about.

Inspiration is available for everyone in some way, and if you haven't found yours yet, follow what is fun for you and you'll find that it starts coming through. It's that spark – a light bulb going off in your head, like an inventor in a cartoon having a eureka moment with a literal light bulb switching on above them. It's a channel of information opening up to you because you're totally in tune with your path of least resistance. Imagine a channel running straight down through your body; any resistance and friction you create narrows that channel, putting blocks in the way and restricting the flow of energy. However, when you're in alignment, that channel is completely open, clear and free, so the energy of inspiration can flow right through you. This means that the more inspiration you're getting, the more in tune with your passions you are.

The inconvenient thing about inspired action is that your guidance will drop in out of absolutely nowhere, probably when you're driving, in the shower or going for a run – basically any time you haven't got your notepad with you! So, as I suggested in the Panorama chapter (*see page 31*), prepare yourself by taking a notepad with you everywhere you go; a small one, with a pen, so you can capture what's coming through. Sometimes, I'll even find that writing is too slow for what I need to catch, so I'll use the voice-note app on my phone instead – and, as I explained, my inspired action comes through writing, so it'll be words, passages and phrases that I'll need to put into a book, blog or post for my @iamLizRoberta Instagram account.

The clearest, but most unexpected thoughts

When I first had the idea for my business, the words that popped into my head didn't make sense at all. I'd recently left my job as a fashion merchandizer and, as I was sitting outside and soaking up the golden morning sunlight, I paused and looked down at the fresh sheet of white paper in front of me. I needed some kind of clarity as to which way to go next on my entrepreneurial journey, because I was finding myself between different new ideas but stuck on where to fully invest my time. So, I tried an exercise that would help me to do just that – the same exercise that I've done at the beginning of every new journal I've started ever since: a page with my name written across the top and a list describing who I am and what I want beneath it.

Intuition in action: get clarity with keywords

On a fresh page of your journal, write your name across the top. This could also be your business name, or pen name if you're an author. Underneath it, write five keywords that embody who you are and/or what you do. Then, write a short paragraph about your future life as if it's happening now. Include the work you're doing, the impact you're having and what you're known for.

Next, write a bullet-point list of five of the biggest future achievements or manifestations you imagine for yourself, such as:

✦ 'I own a detached home.'

✦ 'I am number one on the *New York Times* bestsellers list.'

✦ 'I am happily married with two children.'

✦ 'I wake up every day knowing that I'm in the right place.'

✦ 'I'm grateful every day for what I have.'

Finally, write about your aspirations for physical appearance and health, and then feel free to add anything else that you're inspired to include. The reason it's best to do this exercise on the front page of your journal is because then you can look at it every morning to help you align with what you most want in your life. Constantly reminding your subconscious that this is the plan will invite in the inspired action that's going to guide you towards it.

When you have clarity on your best possible vision of where you want to go, then the inspiration you get is guiding you towards exactly that. That's why it's so important to follow it, and that's why it's so important to have total clarity on what your ideal end result is. Step 1: have clarity on where you want to go. Step 2: follow the inspired action, as it's going to take you there in the easiest and fastest way possible.

When I did this exercise, it began like this: my name went down, followed by five keywords that I wanted to embody. 1) 'Author' (note that this was in 2018, more than two years before I actually signed my first book deal). 2) 'Spiritual Entrepreneur'. *Excuse me?* I had no idea what this meant! Back in 2018, this wasn't a phrase I'd ever seen or heard before. In fact, putting those two words together almost felt sacrilegious, as though the two things were polar opposites that weren't allowed to sit next to each other in the same sentence. You were either spiritual *or* an entrepreneur. I couldn't imagine a business tycoon such as Lord Alan Sugar sitting over a crystal ball with a dreamcatcher and zodiac tapestry pinned up behind him. The words didn't seem to fit together, but they popped into my head – and if you've ever felt that intuitive hit that's like a lightning bolt striking you from the sky, then you know that you need to trust it.

I had no idea how I would be able to make an income from choosing a spiritual career. All the ways I'd made money up until this point were in jobs – either paid by the hour or through an annual salary – and then selling products online. I didn't fully trust the inspiration I was getting, and I hadn't yet learned enough about intuition to know that these hits that drop in are exactly right. You get them because you're supposed to do something with them. The Universe is handing you a seed to grow into something special, and it's probably going to give you the exact result you've been wishing for.

I loved spirituality so much and, I guess, another part of the problem was that I didn't truly believe I'd be able to make a full-time career and income simply from doing what I loved. Spirituality was always a hobby to me, whereas in all the jobs I'd done I had been run-down, miserable and exhausted. Going to work was always something that I dreaded and tried to get away from as much as possible, whereas spirituality was something that I was attracted to and instead had to pull myself *away* from.

One of my core beliefs was that making money had to be hard and so work felt like exactly that: work. To be able to make money from what I loved was the ultimate dream, but one that I didn't believe I was worthy of living. Thankfully, this inspiration that dropped in was the start of me trying to wrap my head around how it could be possible and how I could make it happen. By following this inspiration, step by step, things started falling into place. With every metaphorical magic bean I picked up, more ideas started to sprout.

Trusting inspiration in the gaps in between

It takes a huge amount of patience and trust to follow sporadic guidance because there will inevitably be gaps between the clues and the magic-bean moments; those eerie moments of uncertain pause between the excitement and the inspiration. It's true that inspiration won't always flow. Especially when we feel down, stressed or have an overly busy schedule, it'll be the first thing to disappear. It can feel counterintuitive that to be able to take more inspired action we need to do less, but it's by being as calm and in tune as possible that we keep our channel open to receive ideas for what our best next steps are.

In the pauses between inspiration, it can be endlessly frustrating – feeling as though we've been abandoned by our greatest gift and our most accurate guidance – but the places where inspiration escapes us can be a signal too, as they can tell us that we're stuck in some kind of resistance. The absence of inspiration is only temporary, and it's then that we need to trust most; that's when we need to honour ourselves and take a step back to regroup our thoughts, get grounded and calm our mind. Getting total clarity on what we want our future to look like – without necessarily knowing how we're going to get there – is how we'll invite inspiration back to us. We don't actually need to know the 'how', as long as we have a clear vision of our ideal end result and follow our passion along the way. The more we follow it, the more it'll come through.

Like anything in spirituality, if you don't trust it or follow it, then it'll inevitably get overtaken by the thoughts in your busy conscious mind and ego. To follow your intuition, you need to start putting it first – above any other thoughts in your mind. The more you put it first and trust it, the more it'll appear, and the better guidance you'll receive. I can understand that just reading these words might not be enough for you to believe and conceive this, so put it into practice. Start to try it for yourself. That's the only way you'll really get evidence of how this all works.

Passionate about a cause

Passion flows best when it's not just about you. There's something innate within our humanity and interconnectedness as souls that lights us up the brightest when we're doing something for the whole. When you do things for others – other people, other animals or the environment – the sense of passion you'll feel for your cause can become all-consuming. Having a purpose greater than you is what will light you up more than anything you might feel when it's only for your own gain. Of course, it's a dream to create things for ourselves, but the impact we can have sparks a special type of passion. We can be passionate about our own lives, but I believe that we're all passionate about something so much more – passionate about the change we can create, and passionate about the positive impact we can have in the world.

If you want to explore what you're most passionate about beyond your own life, read back through the earlier chapters on Problems, Panorama and Protest, because they'll have already given you some clues about what this specific area of focus could be for you. Whatever lights you up and lifts your spirit higher is the thing that will inspire you and supply you with endless amounts of passion and purpose. When you get in tune with life in this way, you'll inspire other people, and this is the ripple effect that we can all create to make the world a better place, showing everyone that life can be fun, free and full of excitement.

Kids know this already, but we forget it as adults. By tuning back in to what feels like play and what we love to do all day, we open up avenues for inspiration and abundance to start flowing. Doing more of what we love is so simple that it seems too good to be true, but we're the ones who get to choose how we live our own life. And we're the ones who choose whether or not we're living in tune.

You're the conductor and creator of your own life

Often, we're taught not to trust the unplanned path of inspiration because we're told to follow the logical route instead. As the conductor and creator of your own life, it's within your power to choose again and harmonize yourself with the things that feel better, easier, more fun and more aligned. There are always more friends, more jobs, more places and more opportunities available. So, whatever feels right for you, you must do. The things we feel excited about and inspired by are the things our intuition is telling us to do more of. They make us feel good for a reason: so that we're attracted to them and enticed to fill our natural place in the world.

It's the flow of following what we love that gives us the freedom to move without friction; to find our next lesson; to be guided to what will benefit us the most. It's by following our inspiration that we flow to where our soul wants us to go. Think of the world's greatest artists, or your favourite musician; were their masterpieces created from a place of thinking they 'should' make them but not really wanting to? Probably not. I'd imagine that Leonardo da Vinci felt an intense need to bring to life something beautiful when he painted the *Mona Lisa*. The same goes for Van Gogh: he didn't cut his own ear off because he wasn't that bothered. It seems like he cared a lot...

When you don't trust yourself or realize how valuable and important your own passions are, you're severely limiting yourself and your potential. Cutting off your inspiration is like cutting off a leg while you're trying to walk somewhere – it makes your journey slower, harder and a lot more painful. The random words and pieces of guidance that come through to you may not add up logically, which is why most people discount them. But if they've come through to you, then they're meant for you.

Noticing the buzzes of joy, the sparks of inspiration and the soul-soothing moments of satisfaction will allow you to glide smoothly towards what you want. When you're inspired by something, you put a magical energy into it that other people are going to feel and hopefully be inspired by too. Do what makes you feel excited. Do what makes you feel inspired. And instead of only being a light for other people to follow, how about being the kind of light that *you* would want to follow? The kind that you feel aligned with and inspired by. Be the version of you that keeps inspiring you to be you.

Journalling questions to go deeper into Passion

✎ What do you most look forward to doing?

✎ When do you feel the most alive and inspired?

✎ What is needed for you to be in a more inspired place?

Pinnacle

Question 13: What are you the best at?

. . . .

*'If we did all the things we are capable of
doing, we would literally astound ourselves.'*

Thomas Edison

As you keep following what feels really, *really* good for you, you'll start to notice what heights you can reach. Endurance only comes from a firm belief that you have it within you to get to the end of something – otherwise, you're much more likely to give up before you ever reach your pinnacle. What inspires you will take you further than pushing and forcing yourself ever will, so once you start to notice when you feel inspired and passionate about a particular thing, you might start to realize that you could really commit to becoming the best at it. This is how the most successful people in any field – actors, athletes, artists – create their most in tune lives: by following their inspiration and feeling that they could nurture what inspired them most into an exceptional skill.

How to find out what you do best

I used the word Pinnacle for this chapter because I do believe that we all have something we can climb to the top of. Finding what you're best at can be done in a few different ways, if you're unsure of where your most enchanting talents lie.

Firstly, you need to think about what's been easy for you to do well in without much effort. Were you someone who could roll up to an English exam without doing any preparation and still get top marks? Were you always able to step out in front of a crowd without any fear, while watching other people around you shaking with stage fright? Were you always amazing at baking or giving advice to friends who were having a hard time? Were you always the person who could make everyone laugh and lighten the mood of a room, making you the class clown and resident comedian of your friendship group?

After taking a good, honest look at when success has come easily for you, the next thing you can do is look around at the results you've had. People can recognize your talents more than you even recognize them yourself sometimes, so think about what other people have drawn attention to in your own skill set. If lots of people have said that you're really good at something, there's a very slim chance that they're all making it up. Pay attention to what people are praising you for because they're probably pointing you towards a part of your purpose that you haven't noticed yourself yet.

For example, if you always got really good grades in a certain type of subject, won awards or were praised for something specific you did at work, these are external signs shining a light on something. This can also happen if you get really good feedback about a particular thing you're doing in your business. When you get good feedback, it could be a message from the Universe speaking through that person, so definitely pay attention if you're hearing the same comments again and again. I'm not the only person this happens to – I've spoken to multiple friends who also have businesses and they've had the same experience. They'd get the same message from people over and over until they realized the next direction they were meant to be taking in their business.

It might be difficult to find out what you're best at if your intuition is trying to guide you towards something that not many other people are doing. It wasn't exactly obvious to me that I was meant to have a spiritual career. No one else around me was doing it or was even interested in spirituality, which made the process incredibly confusing. It was a lonely experience as I realized I had to go down a path that wasn't yet widely accepted. The thing you're the best at could be something very different to a lot of other people around you, because your purpose is to be more of you, which might mean being less like everyone else.

There are other challenges that can come up when you're trying to figure out what this thing is for you, and this question is going to feel extremely difficult for some people to answer. If you're one of the people who saw Question 13 and thought: 'I have absolutely *no* idea... I'm rubbish at everything!', then there's probably some low self-esteem clouding the truth of your intuition. Your intuition is your line of connection to your true soul self, who knows that you were born perfect, divine and flawless. When you see yourself as anything other than that, you're not seeing clearly to the truth of who you are.

Another way to find out what you're the best at is by noticing what you're *not* the best at. Through this process of elimination, you can tune out those things that aren't getting you the results you want, aren't making an impact and aren't making you feel good about yourself – and tune in more to the things that are paying off.

I don't feel like I need to explain this one too much because we all know when we're not great at something: it feels like a struggle, it feels hard, and our intuition is telling us to do anything but this thing that we're not very good at. Sometimes we can start off pretty bad at something because we're new to it, but our intuition tells us to practise so that we do become good at it. However, if we have absolutely no desire whatsoever to practise, and just want to get the hell away from it and never do it again, then it's something to cross off the list because it's probably not what we're ever going to be the best at.

Intuition in action: feelings in the body (good)

As much as you can feel in your body when something is bad (see page 53), you can definitely feel when something is good. When inspiration lights you up, it can physically jolt you, making your head twitch or giving you a full-body shudder. When you get a great idea popping into your head out of nowhere, you might get chills on your body that make your hairs stand on end as a sign of confirmation. It will almost be like a jolt of electricity pulsing through your entire nervous system and waking something up within you.

That energy that excites you is a bolt of bodily intuition. It may come through as an emotional feeling of elation or excitement that makes your heart beat faster. It might feel like a fizzing sense of anticipation in your stomach, rather than the drop and dread you'd feel there if your intuition was guiding you away from something. Overall, you'll just feel really, *really* good in your body when you're being guided towards something by your intuition.

You'll feel uplifted, lighter and full of vitality. You'll have energy to initiate something and then carry on with it. You'll have a natural boost of motivation and resilience. You might even find it hard to sleep because you're completely wired and full of ideas. Whatever sparks this response in you is absolutely in tune with who you truly are and what you love to do. If you can align your life with more of these good feelings, then everything will start to flow.

Whatever feelings you get when you're having fun are the same feelings you'll get in your body when you're doing what feels fulfilling. It will feel like a sense of satisfaction, as though there's nowhere else you need or want to be right now. Your body will be at peace because you are. As a soul in your body, you're one and the same, and when there's a mismatch between what you're doing and how you feel, it's a sign that something is out of tune – and, therefore, it's a sign for you to move on and make a change.

....

10,000 hours

I don't know if it really will take 10,000 hours to reach your pinnacle, but it'll probably take a lot of time and a lot of practice, as that's how anyone reaches the pinnacle of anything. Inspired action will light up what this particular area is for you, but it's always up to you to commit each part of yourself – your mind, body and spirit – to reaching your fullest potential, where your greatest sense of purpose will be waiting for you.

Nurturing your natural home of inspiration will take you to new places you've never been before. If you want to become an expert in something or go further than anyone has ever been, it's essential that it's something that inspires you – otherwise the process will become so agonizing and frustrating that you won't be able to carry on with it. However, if you're following your inspired action and embracing something you're passionate about, the prospect of pursuing it until you reach the pinnacle will become an opportunity you feel compelled to chase.

You can reach the top, if it's a mountain you actually want to climb. Feelings of wanting to give up will come and go, but if you can feel a sense of potential within you, it's there to take form and turn into something so that you can have a better life. If you can let yourself believe that you could become great at something, you might just prove it true. You might need to let go of any lies or illusions that the best spaces are only reserved for other people; there's always one reserved for you, because it's one that only you can fill.

Client case study: something inside to spiritual guide

My client Colleen was a small Scottish lady with a heart full of love and a smile to match. She literally radiated joy and was incredibly skilled at writing and teaching in the most compassionate way. When we started working together, she was already having success teaching yoga and hosting monthly moon circles, with a membership society to boot. However, she wanted to grow, expand and make the full impact that she knew she was capable of making. On one of our calls, she inspired me by saying: 'I just know I have this potential within me, and I can't explain it – but I know this is what I'm meant to be doing.'

That certainty and clarity about the path she wanted to be on inspired her to keep learning, keep working and keep putting many hours into her growing spiritual business, seven days a week. It meant that people were starting to notice her, and that she was building a community of clients who raved about her work and listened to her teachings. As anyone who starts a spiritual business online knows, it's not like you hop on to Instagram stories and YouTube on your first day, filming yourself talking completely naturally and openly. It always takes practice, and the people you think do it well have probably been practising for years beforehand. By the time Colleen had invested in working with me, she was already well under way and making amazing progress, so she was over the first and hardest hurdle.

However, she wanted to show herself more and step into the role of the spiritual teacher that she really was. She wanted to fully embody the place that she knew inside she was here to fill, and she wanted to align with her favourite topic of teaching: yogi philosophy. It was this strong belief – that there was something inside telling her to be a spiritual guide – which enabled her to keep going because her intuition told her she had the chance to be really great at it. She knew this was how she could make the biggest impact, and when we feel that we have something inside, we can all allow that to be our guide, until we find out what we're really capable of.

You can excel and exceed expectations

By noticing what you're best at, you can be successful so much more easily. You can create the impact you have in your heart to make and touch so many more lives by simply doing what comes easily to you. When you think about it, that's why it's so much easier to create massive material wealth and abundance this way, by capitalizing on what you can do best. People will be more willing to pay for your skills and ask for your help if they can see that you're exceptionally good at something. I bet if you think of your favourite celebrities or sportspeople, you can see why they've got to the top of their field – it's because they found what they were the best at and then they practised and carried on with it until everyone else could see that they were the best too.

I don't know about you, but I always get incredibly inspired by people who have reached the pinnacle of their career – like Arnold Schwarzenegger, who conquered the heights of bodybuilding and then Hollywood, before becoming the Governor of California. Needless to say, we're probably going to be most inspired by people who are in the exact field that we want to be in – but anyone who has done something exceptional is inspirational, nonetheless. The commitment it takes is something to be applauded, but beyond that, their trust in their own talent is perhaps even more important. Our belief in ourselves and our own intuition is the thing that will carry us towards our purpose and to the highest heights of where it can take us.

Tuning in to this is a lot easier when you find out where your natural confidence lies, and what you're most passionate about and inspired by. Once you've figured out these pieces, you'll feel like a potential timeline opens up in front of you where you really could reach the top of something because you have everything you need to carry you there. Knowing what you're best at and riding the wave that you already have some natural momentum behind will allow you to flow more smoothly towards the best results possible. Your intuition always wants to take you down the easiest and most aligned route, and the path of least resistance will be open to you once you're not working against your natural talents.

Regardless of what other people are doing, your job is only to find out what you're the best at within your own life because it might be totally unique and different to what anyone else around you is doing. You can excel and exceed your expectations if you do what excites you and what you know plays to your natural strengths. You can be the best if you want to be, you just need to decide what feels most in tune and easy for you. Trust in your intuition to keep guiding you because, as you pay attention to what it's pointing you towards, this process will become easier as you grow more aware of what your special skill is and what it feels like. Be true to you by trusting your talents and doubt your limits instead of your potential.

Journalling questions to go deeper into Pinnacle

🖋 What are your natural gifts?

🖋 What have people always told you you're good at?

🖋 How can you use your talents more effectively?

Path

Question 14: How has your journey shaped who you are?

....

*'Failure is a great teacher, and if you are open
to it, every mistake has a lesson to offer.'*
Oprah Winfrey

Your job while you're here will be revealed to you, in part, by the journey that has shaped you. Whether the path you've been on for the last few years was planned or not, it will have taken you along twists and turns that revealed deeper parts of you and strengthened your ability to cope with change and uncertainty. If your path had been straight all along, you wouldn't have learned as much, and with the gift of hindsight, you can usually see that the unexpected path you ended up on was the best one for you in the end.

Designing your destiny

Going back to the conversation we had about power when we first started this journey together, it's within your power to choose your path – and it's also in your power to see how your previous path can be of benefit to you. While you may have been a victim of something on your path previously, you don't still have to be a victim of it in the future. You can transform it into something so much bigger and better, making the path in front of you endlessly brighter. The path you're on can be one that's in pursuit of a sense of purpose, and I'd strongly assume that's your aim, as you've chosen to buy this book and read it up to this point so far.

So, at this exact point on your path, when you're reading this chapter and thinking about this question, you have this decision to make. You can decide what path you're going to make for yourself going forwards based on everything you've gained and experienced so far. Maybe one of the big lessons you learned was that you always need to listen to your intuition to find the most fulfilling way to go next. I've already told you how this was the case for me and how I ended up in careers that felt awful at the time because I didn't listen to my intuition. They were the wake-up calls I needed to make me notice and choose differently next time.

For you, it might be in love, if you keep ending up with the same type of person every time, somehow expecting a different outcome. Or it could be to do with any other area of your life, such as having money issues or not finding friends you can trust. If you take yourself along a path that doesn't intuitively feel fully right, there are two ways you can get back on track: either the Universe will take you there because it's sick of waiting, or you can take the reins and choose to do differently. One of these options is far less painful than the other, and I don't think I need to tell you which one it is.

If you stay still for too long when it doesn't feel right, you might eventually get moved by forces out of your control.

Don't think that you have to stay suspended and motionless because you can't decide which path you should be taking. Just move forwards and then see what happens; you'll know what's right or wrong for you in the way you feel. If you have a nagging feeling that this isn't the path you're meant to be on at all, you'll know that it's your time to take a detour. If so, please know that you have the ability to guide yourself forwards with your intuition. That's literally what it's there for. You can use all of the methods I've given so far in this book to help you with this, and if you need specific guidance on which way to go next, you can also use a pendulum...

Intuition in action: using a pendulum

No one really knows how a pendulum gets its answers, but I believe that it's micro-movements in our muscles responding in the same way that they do in the muscle testing exercise (*see page 5*).

To use this method, you could buy a crystal pendulum (these are usually a quartz point, but I have a lovely obsidian one), which will be a pointed crystal on the end of a line of chain. However, you can also use a necklace just as well – or anything else that's a weight on the end of a piece of thread or metal chain.

Rest your elbow on a table and put your hand up in the air, as though your arm is making the shape of a 'V' with your elbow at the bottom point of it. Put your pendulum on the end of your forefinger and wait for it to stop swinging. Say out loud (or in your mind), 'Pendulum, show me which way you swing for "yes"', and note the direction. Then let it hang still before saying, 'Pendulum, show me which way you swing for "no"' and notice how it swings in the opposite direction. Once you've got those answers, you can start asking the questions that you want to have a 'yes' or 'no' answer to. If you get a clockwise motion for 'yes' and your pendulum starts swinging clockwise for your answer, then that's your guidance.

However you believe the pendulum works, I think any tool like this is extremely useful for giving you confirmation of what you really want the answer to be. You might think you're not sure about something, but when you're told 'no' find that you're disappointed because you actually wanted the answer to be 'yes'. So, whichever answer your pendulum gives you, notice how you feel and what you sense when you tune in to the answer. Using a pendulum is a quick and easy way to get 'yes' or 'no' guidance to simple questions.

....

The most important thing is that you keep moving forwards while your path continues to take shape. In action, we open ourselves up to opportunity. In inaction, we become inert. Even if you don't know what you want, by moving forwards you'll still be able to feel when you're getting closer or further away from it. Your own story is a unique gift to you based on the individual journey you've been on, and by honouring it, you'll start to see the sacred wisdom of your soul. Don't ever get downhearted because you think that other people's paths have been smoother than yours. Your path was designed with you in mind, and it has been perfect for you to learn everything that you need to know so far.

Twists and turns during your time here

Each and every detour is magnificent in its own way because, as you meander through life, you collect a wide breadth of experiences that make you into a wiser and more well-rounded person. If you've had a very long and winding path in your life so far, I don't want you to think that this says anything bad about you; in fact, there are countless good things you can take from every twist and turn you've experienced. In the baby-boomer days, it was encouraged to have a single, secure job for your whole adult life, so that you could buy a house with a white picket fence to put your feet up in every evening and weekend because you'd 'made it'.

However, in the generations since, due to the advent of the internet, cheap holidays and Instagram envy as a result of seeing strangers living lives that look better than ours, more recent generations know that there are so many other options available. These options can feel overwhelming, like there's too much to choose from, and yet we never know what each option is really going to be like until we do it. This can mean that we try on many different hats and multiple different types of lifestyle before we settle into the one that feels the best for us. Everyone has a path that's unique to them and, when we start to look around, we'll see that everyone's path is interesting in some way. The people who are the most heavily tuned in to their purpose have often had the most interesting journeys of all.

You may have become an expert in many different things through the twists and turns your life has taken, and this is no bad thing. What you've walked away from helps you to know what you're walking towards. Even when you can't see how things are meant to be, you can see what they were and who you were. From there, you have the option to decide which way you want to go forwards. Let yourself loose from the idea that things should have been perfect so far – maybe they were, but in a different way than you expected.

If life were only to reveal to us what we already know to be true, we might just stay in comfort and continue on as we are, missing the chance to explore those parts of ourselves that are hidden beneath that surface level. It's only through the unanticipated moments and events that our soul self really has the chance to shine through. They show us where we have a chance to grow, as well as where we have hidden resilience and a vast array of tools in our emotional toolkit to help us navigate challenges. Feeling the full range of emotions is what allows us to tune in more intelligently to what our intuition feels like.

Imagine if you hadn't had much experience of your emotions. It would be very hard to distinguish the tiny details and intricate indicators that come through your body and feelings when your intuition is speaking to you. By knowing what feels bad, you know what you want to avoid in the future. By knowing what feels good, you know what you want more of in the future. This is how your path works – and this is how you're able to guide yourself along it. There are many timelines available to you. You get to choose which way you go forwards, and which fate you want for your time here. Do you want to stay on the path you're on? Or do you want to make a change today and choose a different one?

Better than expected

One of the most magical things that many people learn while travelling along their path in life is that things will often turn out better than expected. Whenever we feel disappointed, it's usually only a matter of time before we're able to understand the reason, because there's something so much better hiding around the corner. It might take many years to realize what this is, and there may be many more lessons to uncover afterwards, until it all ties together to create a big vision picture of how everything worked out even better than we could have possibly imagined.

As someone who's been on many different paths, both in life and in my career, I can say that you'll definitely know when you're finally in tune with your highest path. However, you'll also be able to look back and see that it probably wouldn't have been possible without the journey you'd taken beforehand. I couldn't guide and teach people about spirituality if I hadn't always felt drawn to the topic and led a life that caused me to develop a deep empathy and inquisitive mind as to why humans behave the way they do. I wouldn't be able to help people with their spiritual careers if I hadn't had so many years in the business world learning about marketing and making a profit. I wouldn't be able to write books if I hadn't had such an insatiable appetite to read so many and find out what I could learn to make my life better.

This is another thing about your unique path: it's tailor-made by you and for you, because your soul is always wanting you to grow, and that's the main aim of your experience here on Earth. In Earth school, the main lesson is to tune in to your intuition and guide yourself to the highest possible potential of what you can fulfil while you're here. When you start to notice where your path has been taking you, it'll make a little more sense. It gets to get better and better. It gets to be easy – and yet still exciting – if you're following your intuition without knowing exactly where it's taking you next. Yet, even when you don't know where it's taking you, you can trust it to always be the best next step it could possibly be for you. Your route gets to be as unique as you are, regardless of the path anyone else has taken before you.

We can look back in horror at the things we used to do before and the terrible decisions we made, or we can choose to use them for a purpose. Obviously, we can't undo the past – but we can use our past to shape our future and make it into one that we're proud of. Our biggest crises can become those critical moments that spun our life onto a completely different path and, ultimately, they can be for the better if we choose to understand the lessons these experiences taught us. There may be trials and tribulations that turn out to be the perfect preparation for living our purpose. A linear life does not lend itself to becoming a wise woman of the world; to learn more and know more, we need to experience more. The path we have already started walking down is exactly the one we need.

Journalling questions to go deeper into Path

🖋 How have you become an expert at something?

🖋 Why has your journey been different to most other people's?

🖋 When has life taken you on a route better than the one you had planned?

Past

Question 15: What lessons have you learned that the world should know?

. . . .

'You've always had the power my dear,
you just had to learn it for yourself.'

Glinda the Good Witch, in *The Wizard of Oz*

I'm sure you've noticed that everyone's journey is unique, and it's part of what makes us all individuals with a different story to tell. When you tell your story and share the lessons you've learned, you have the chance to help someone through their most challenging times or to enlighten them with the information that you wish you'd once known. When something is telling you to teach and share a certain message, it's because there's a deep sense of fulfilment to be found for you when you're using the lessons from your own journey to help guide other people along theirs.

The wise storytellers

The people who are the best storytellers often have the most interesting personal story to tell, with many tales behind them that they've turned into something to teach. Challenging yourself to teach more, be more and do more may not have always been your plan; but when life has taken you on such an interesting journey, why wouldn't you want to share what you've learned? When you know how something can be done in a better way and you're aware of the positive impact it could have, it almost becomes a compulsion that you need more people to know about it. What you've become a master of in your own life is wisdom that other people may need right now.

You might never consider yourself to be a teacher until the right thing comes up that you know you need to talk about. This is about so much more than being a teacher in the traditional 'school' sense; this is about being a messenger of truth, a container of wisdom and an example of what could be possible by choosing a different path. If your intuition is telling you that your past has been for a purpose, as though you've already been given exactly what you need to take your most aligned next steps, then what time has taught you can be a valuable lesson that you go on to teach others.

Your past can hold you back or it can guide you further forwards. The choice is always yours and, to know which one to make, you need to realize what will make you feel like your time on Earth has been spent in a better way. Do you want to be the person who knew something important but kept it to themselves? Or do you want to be the one who created a change that reached far beyond you? Looking back on your life as a reflective exercise can help you to see what you were made for and what you're meant for. To tune in to what this is, you'll need to reflect on your past and take note of what you find.

Intuition in action: joining the dots to the past

This is an exercise that I'm sure, to be honest, most people would rather avoid – but I'm going to put it here anyway because it will help you. Especially if your past has been painful, it can be so much easier to bury it, forget it and move on. But there are crucial lessons in there that may be full of purpose if you can bring them out and transmute them into something that's helpful for others.

Sit in a quiet place with your journal and give yourself some time alone. Take a deep breath and write down a big life-changing event from your past. Then, underneath, list the following:

✦ Describe the biggest lesson you've learned from the event that has now made your life better.

✦ What advice would you have for someone going through a similar experience?

✦ Would you be willing to talk about it and share this lesson with the people who need it?

You can repeat this process for each big, life-changing event from your past that you can think of. Again, it may be uncomfortable to revisit events in your past that were hard at the time, but you can always find a sense of purpose if you're fully ready to look for it. By joining the dots to the past, you can find out what your own biggest lessons were to see what you were taught and can now teach others.

You learn lessons by living them so that you can pass them on to whoever else needs them. You have experienced so much, which in turn allows you to give so much. How you want to serve the world is probably how you wish you were once saved yourself. When you feel a compulsion to share and educate about something that you know would give others the help they need, it could be a part of your calling that's compelling you through the inner nudges of your intuition.

What your intuition has taught you

From our past, we learn so much about our intuition. We learn what we like and what we don't like. We learn from our mistakes, like when we had a bad gut feeling but went with it anyway. We learn from the times when we felt that something was going to come true and it did. A powerful way to connect with your intuition is to realize all the times it's been with you in the past.

How you connect with your own unique intuition is something that only you can fully figure out, but it's been with you all along, which means that your past is a very important key to awakening your intuition. Some people may have vivid dreams that connect them with the people or answers they need, or feel a certain connection with their soul through writing. Some experience sounds or sensations in their ears; for me, it's the sound of a bell ringing, but I've also worked with a deaf client who experienced it as her ear getting hotter when something was true. Most people aren't trained to notice these subtle senses, but you're not most people.

By analysing when your intuitive senses have alerted you in the past, you can build better awareness of how your intuition works during the decisions you need to make now and in the future. Just as I've used everything I've learned from my past to now teach about spirituality and using your intuition, you'll also have lessons that you're able to share for the benefit of others.

Every individual on this Earth is a memory bank of different lessons and experiences, so we just need to understand what we've learned and what we want to leave behind as our legacy. We teach our children, we teach our parents (as my mum said to me) and we teach our partners about love. Passing on knowledge to someone else to make their life better is incredibly fulfilling, hence the sense of purpose it brings. What often holds us back from being a teacher is a belief that we have nothing of value worth saying, or that we have nothing to teach. I had to face all of this when I realized that I was being called to be an author because some deep fears started rising up.

Not because of the writing – I loved writing and it was always the easiest thing for me at school – but because of the speaking. What most people don't realize is that a large part of being a non-fiction author is everything that you do outside of your books: the speaking engagements, the workshops and the teaching. These were all a bit scary for me. I had an intense fear of speaking publicly and any presentations I'd ever had to give at school, university or work had sent me into a state of paralysing panic. I had major imposter syndrome because I was scared that people would think I was boring or not saying anything interesting.

Another thing that I thought would prevent me from ever being able to teach is my introversion. I find presenting to be hugely energy-draining, and to be honest, so is being around people for too long! This is why I want you to know that it's safe for you to take the next steps that you feel compelled to take while moving towards a more in tune life, even when you're not entirely sure that you have what it takes yet. As so many people don't trust their feelings enough, they fear the calling rather than following it. But if you feel like your time for something new has come, it's because you've already learned the lessons you need to know. You only ever get what you're ready for – and when you have learned enough and it's time for you to teach, your students will appear.

When the teacher is ready...

My students literally did appear. A whole classroom, in fact. Three seminar groups full, to be precise. Three months after leaving my career in fashion, I got the annual email from the head of course on my old master's degree, Mike: 'I don't suppose you'd be able to come down and give the students a guest lecture about buying and merchandizing, would you?' Every year since I graduated I got the same request, and every year I politely turned it down. The idea of using one of my 21 days' holiday to drive a six-hour round trip and give a voluntary guest lecture was anything but tempting.

But he never gave up, and by the third time he asked me, I no longer had to worry about using up my scant holiday days, as I'd left full-time work to pursue my dreams of becoming a spiritual entrepreneur and author. I did, however, still have an all-consuming fear of public speaking, so as I chewed on my lip and mulled the invitation over in my mind, a few days passed before I was ready to open the email again and press 'reply'. If you have this fear too, you'll know the avoidance tactics that pop in to save you from a potential fall from grace in front of a live audience. Maybe I could bring in a partner so I'd only have to speak half as much? Maybe I could say I'm trapped overseas and only available for a teleconference via Zoom? Or maybe I'll just send an email write-up of everything I know. Wouldn't that be better?

Unfortunately, he was expecting me to be there, in person, all alone behind a wooden podium, with 150 sets of eyes on me from the tiered layers of auditorium seating. After agreeing to commit and wrestling with my regret in the last days leading up to it, I saved my PowerPoint onto a pink USB stick I still had stashed in a pencil case from my degree days, and practised in front of my iPhone. The date we had decided on was Monday, 13 May – the day after my birthday. This made sense in terms of the logistics because I would be in my home town seeing family for my birthday that weekend anyway, and the campus was en route back to our house halfway up the country. I packed a bag and pushed down my nerves somewhere beneath my toiletry bag and pairs of pants.

The campus was somewhere I was always happy to be. The buildings on either side of the street were separated by two rows of towering trees that looked as majestic in autumn as they did in spring. At the end of the road was a park with a river that looked like an idyllic vision of how you'd imagine the English countryside to be. There were ducks swimming, fallen green leaves floating on top of the stream as it babbled gently over the pebbles underneath, and parents eating pastries on benches as their children played on the grass. I wore my best dress that said I was formal yet fashionable, which is a harder thing to achieve than you might think.

The speech went better than I expected despite me being a ball of nerves. As I started talking, the rhythm started to flow, and the practice that I'd put in at home on my own seemed to pay off. The students appeared to be engaged, and the fact that they were putting their hands up at the end to ask questions told me that they'd been listening and taking in the information. Afterwards, Mike greeted me at the entrance and we caught up on the past three years over coffee in the cafeteria. He was a gentle giant with a posh English accent – the kind that said he'd come from the Home

Counties with ample years of high-quality education behind him. His long, white-grey hair bounced as he turned his head to one side and rested his chin on his hand, contemplating something before he said it. As he turned his head back to look at me from behind his black spectacles, he said that he had an offer for me: 'Hmm... that was good. I don't know how you'll feel about this, but do you want a job?'

With a generous hourly rate that was far more than I'd ever earned per hour before, combined with the fact that the job was part-time, which meant no cutting back on my dreams was required, I said that I'd think about it but get back to him in the next few days. I smiled in the spring sun as I walked quickly to meet Ally and my mum for a belated birthday lunch. None of us could believe it! But when I look back on the opportunity that was given to me that day to start working as a university marketing lecturer, I realize that it was only possible because I'd leaped and then leaped again.

When I started teaching on the same master's degree programme that I'd been on three years before, I was a trembling wreck of nerves. After my first two days of standing up in front of a classroom of students, I knew that the way I was feeling at the end of the day wasn't right. I was extremely fatigued from the cortisol that had been pulsing through my veins, both on the day I was teaching and on the day beforehand, when I was anticipating teaching. I took myself off to hypnotherapy, which I'd had for generalized anxiety disorder already, and it helped to take the edge off.

As with anything, I got better and more comfortable over time, and through that job I was able to learn another lesson I'd need for the rest of my career as an author and teacher of spirituality. Speaking is something that I'll have to do for the rest of my life, and this job was the perfect practice I needed before stepping behind a podium in front of much larger rooms full of people with much greater expectations and tickets in their hands.

Moments weave together to craft the toolkit you need to complete your mission in the world, so trust that everything you've learned is of enormous value because it can be. Regardless of how many lessons you have left to learn, there are lessons you've already learned that the world needs to know. What you feel compelled to share is a part of your calling that's waiting for you to step up and answer it. What you've learned could make someone else's path smoother, easier, less painful or more joyful. Your wisdom is unique to you and only you know the lessons you need to share, but the most important thing is that you do – so that the rest of the world can know it too.

Journalling questions to go deeper into Past

🖋 Can you remember when you had a strong sense of intuition about something?

🖋 What happened – did you follow it or not?

🖋 Who are you meant to teach and how?

Present

Question 16: What activity brings you fully into the present moment?

....

'Life gives you plenty of time to do whatever you want to do if you stay in the present moment.'

Deepak Chopra

A state of surrender is a sign that you're willing to be wherever you're meant to be and that you'll allow your intuition to lead your life forwards. Noticing the moments when time loses all meaning because you're not trying to escape is just as important as noticing the moments that you can't wait to get away from. Whatever is happening in your life right now, by fully accepting what is already there you can find huge clues about what's in store for your future. By allowing yourself to receive the full experience of every moment as it's happening, you can reach the full range of intuitive insights that are always available to you, as long as you're ready to enter each moment as it already is.

The difference between be-ing and do-ing

Sometimes hustle is required. I definitely can't claim that I never have those days when I start work at 5 a.m. and finish at 10 p.m. or something similar. Modern life is *oh so busy*, especially if you have a family, one or more jobs, and/or a business of your own. But whatever is going on in your life, your moments are limited and it's up to you to make the most of each one as it comes. Your time is entirely yours, so you get to decide how you approach your moments and what you get out of them.

Whatever your current situation is, you can find some sense of connection with yourself in each moment if you move into a mindset of be-ing rather than do-ing. To be able to do this is simply a case of realizing where you're focusing your energy. Even if the activity doesn't change, you can switch between these two modes. Be-ing means that you're fully enveloped in who you are in each moment, soaking it all in and seeing what good can be found there. On the other hand, do-ing is like leaving yourself because your energy is entirely outside of your body in the task, rather than being connected to the centred part of you.

When we devote our lives entirely to do-ing, we may look back and wonder where it went. We might feel as though we missed out, and therefore feel a sense of regret and remorse because we wish we could have appreciated things more. This can happen when someone we love dies – we wish we had savoured their laugh, enjoyed their company for a little bit longer and soaked up each minute of the time we spent with them. By being conscious of the present moment and committing to it, we can invest all of our energy into fully experiencing life, while avoiding the risk of regretting any moments we weren't fully present for.

If you find yourself always feeling run-down and stressed, that's definitely a strong sign that you're in a busy state of do-ing rather than be-ing. Anxiety and stress are enemies of intuition because they can completely close your channel of intuitive information. The mind becomes so loud and hectic that your brain is completely overwhelmed and there's just no way you can hear your true feelings and intuitive thoughts beneath it. If you haven't connected with your intuition yet, this could be a big reason why. It's the most common one that I see in people – and again, this could well be a symptom of having a busy life with so much on your plate. In which case, there are ways that you can still honour yourself while fulfilling all of the responsibilities you have. One way to do this is with mindfulness...

Intuition in action: mindfulness in the moment

Without even changing your situation at all, you can be more mindful and step into a state of be-ing rather than do-ing. Mindfulness means that you're totally embodying and accepting yourself in whatever you're doing, whether it's driving, cooking, working, socializing or exercising. It means that you're entirely aware of every sensation you're feeling and every emotion that's coming up. It means that you're tuning in fully and not missing out on anything, soaking up what's happening in you and around you, and surrendering entirely to the present moment.

Next time you're doing an activity such as:

+ bathing the kids

+ running in the park

✦ cooking dinner

✦ or walking somewhere in the sunshine

take a second to move your awareness out of your brain and into your body, so that you can see what you're experiencing outside of your mind's chatter. To do this:

✦ Notice what sounds are around you. Can you hear the sound of waves? People laughing or talking? Wind blowing? Or a pot bubbling on a stove?

✦ Notice what you see. Where is the light reflecting from? What colours are vivid around you? Are there any possessions near you that you treasure?

✦ Notice what you can touch or feel. What textures are you surrounded by? Is it hot or cold? What feels soft, smooth or rough?

✦ Notice your thoughts. Is your mind running fast or slow? How many thoughts do you have going on at once? Are you tired or focused? Are you easily finding the positives or the negatives?

✦ Notice your emotions. Are you feeling peaceful or stressed? Is there something outside of the present moment affecting your emotional state, like something that's happened in the past or something that you're anticipating in the near future?

Noticing each moment more will mean that you don't miss them, and it will reveal to you how much pleasure can be found by fully experiencing what's already around you. Adding your intention into everything you're doing will instantly make your actions feel more purposeful for you, as though you're bringing your full self to them without needing to change either yourself or what you're doing to be able to enjoy them.

....

Surrendering to the moment we're already in

A lot of our resistance rises up because we're trying to get out of the moment we're in. The way that we can always surrender without even changing our external situation at all is by letting everything be what it already is. Of course, this is a lot easier said than done, but with practice we'll find that it becomes easier, as we allow life to flow past us and through us while staying completely centred and grounded in who we authentically are.

Surrendering to the moment means knowing what you can change and what you can't change, and respecting the full power that you have while not wishing to be anyone different. Making peace with yourself and the place you're in is how you can surrender to life, and it's where you will find the most blissful state of satisfaction that's always available.

Control is trying to force ourselves to resist the natural flow, and when we're so certain about staying stuck, we're going to ignore our intuition when it's telling us we need to move. A constant state of doing keeps us busy and enables us to avoid having to listen to our thoughts, feel our true feelings and make different decisions that could completely disrupt our life. Our intuitive thoughts and feelings could be telling us that everything is wrong and out of tune, so it's often easier to tune *those* out instead of adjusting our life to make things right for us.

A lot of issues around control stem from a fear of surrendering. This is especially likely if you have a background of trauma or a chaotic upbringing that might make you feel as though everything could unravel at any moment if you're not actively holding it all together yourself. The only way to get past this is to prove yourself wrong, and to show your brain that it's only a belief – because the reality is that when you surrender and let go, life is even more magical than when you're holding on to the past or wishing for the future.

We need to be totally open to experiencing what's available now if we want to receive our intuitive insights. Letting go emotionally, mentally and energetically is the best way to show that we're fully ready to receive what our intuition wants to tell us. Space and surrender create a fertile bed for inspiration to bloom, and by stopping and being still, we allow it to come in creatively in ways we couldn't have predicted. Being content with a mental vacuum and not always knowing what's coming next is how your intuition will thrive.

When are you checking out?

If you find that you're checking out of more moments than you'd like, decide to be more intentional and take yourself deeper into the moments all around you so that you don't miss them. It's up to you how much you choose to savour the life you already have, even if there are changes your intuition is telling you to make. Not resisting anything – including what you already have right now – is the best way to move forwards.

It can feel uneasy to surrender to a present moment that we don't want to be in, which is why we often avoid it. But acceptance is where the change starts. When we notice what we have now, what feels good and what we want to be different, we're catching up with ourselves and stopping the separation. It's not possible to resist the present moment until we get to the future. It's only by fully entering the present moment that we can create the future we want.

If you can create a lifestyle where you have regular check-in points throughout your day to empty your mind and tune in to your intuition, it'll help you to gain a lot more clarity while also getting used to what the present moment really feels like. There will be some activities that help you to get into the present moment more than others. It might be the things you do at the end of the day to unwind (like when I used to get home from my day in the office and watch videos about spirituality all evening), or it could be whatever you're doing when time loses all meaning because you're so absorbed in the task at hand.

If you don't know what brings you into the present moment yet, all you need to do is start to observe, notice and feel when control is slipping away and a calm satisfaction slips in instead. One of my favourite actors, Jennifer Aniston, talked about this feeling when she was sat on the sofa opposite Oprah in 2005. By the time she was speaking with the almighty O, she was one of the highest-paid female actors in Hollywood. What Jennifer Aniston talked about in her interview was something that she'd experienced for the first time after doing yoga with a close friend. A moment of total peace and satisfaction washed over her, and she turned and said to her friend: 'I'm feeling a feeling I don't know if I've ever actually felt before, and that is that I don't want to be anywhere other than where I am right now.' She continued on to say that this meant not dwelling on the past or obsessing about something in the future: 'It was a feeling of total peace.'[5].

The moments we're missing out on might be the ones giving us the biggest intuitive clues. The ones we don't want to be present for might be indicators we're ignoring that are telling us something is out of tune. When we're in tune, there's nowhere else we'd rather be than the present moment – instead of wanting to avoid, ignore or escape it. When we notice the times, places and activities that make us want to settle into the stillness and float with nowhere to go, this is when we're connecting with the truest version of ourselves. When we're in tune, we're in flow and we're glad to be exactly where we are in the here and now.

Remember to float...

The river of ease and flow is one that most of us are not sailing on. We hope that once we reach a certain place or a certain goal, *then* it will be smooth sailing. However, when we tune in to the things that make us want to swim in the stillness and float without moving anywhere, they're the activities that bring us into the present moment and they're the things that will make us feel full and content. There is nothing wrong with wanting to pursue more; as the Universe constantly expands, so can we – but that doesn't mean that amidst our expansion and growth we should lose the joy in the current moment.

By having gratitude for all that we've created so far, we bring the present moment to life and we honour the journey we've already been on. In the minutes and moments when we keep moving, moving, moving, without taking a pause to breathe and feel grateful for what already is, we're missing out on the light moments of surrender that create a state of true ease and flow. When we find what we can stay still in, without an itch that we can only scratch by moving forwards, we are already there – in the presence of our purpose.

If you don't know where you want to go, notice what you don't want to get away from in your current life. Your present is another clue to your purpose, and by tuning in to the things that you're happy to stay with, your intuition is telling you that you've already found something perfectly in tune for you. In the stillness that lives inside the seconds we're always busy rushing between, we can reach what our intuition is always trying to connect us to: the end state of us being us.

Journalling questions to go deeper into Present

🖉 What do you want to keep about your current life?

🖉 What activities make you stop watching the clock?

🖉 Are you ready to start surrendering to the present moment?

Patience

Question 17: What means enough to you that you'd be willing to wait for it?

....

*'Nature does not hurry, yet
everything is accomplished.'*

Lao Tzu

If we think something is worth waiting for, then it's probably because we place a lot of value on it and know that it's going to add to our life in some way. Whether it's something that's going to make us happier, healthier, richer, freer or all of the above, it must be important if we're able to wait for a long period of time while still keeping our goal in sight. When we're rushing towards things, the panic comes from a place of scarcity because we don't think we'll get them without force and without controlling the timeline. This is another way that we need to let go: by not only being willing to stay in the present moment, but also knowing that the future will unfold in perfect timing.

In your own time

The rush is another way that we keep ourselves stuck. When we're trying to chase down a timeline, we could be taking the harder route instead of allowing our intuition to lead us to exactly what we want. Once we've experienced this a few times it becomes obvious – the confidence of knowing our desire, the calm sense of acceptance that it's going to happen as we co-create with the Universe, and the smooth process of following the signs, invitations and inspiration.

Those things that it seems you have to grasp and grab at to keep are not the things that are flowing effortlessly into your life. Therefore, it's a major hint that you're hot in pursuit of something you don't truly feel is meant for you. Think of that feeling you have when you think time is running out. How does it feel? Good? No. It makes your heart race faster, and the likelihood is that you feel a bit panicky and stressed. Is this the sign of an intuitively led life lived in tune? Also, no.

There are many things that can make us feel like this, but the majority of them live only in our own mind. Our limiting beliefs tell us why things are scarce, why there's not enough of x, y and z, and why we simply *must* have it now or forever suffer the consequences without it. It's not our intuition telling us these things, but rather the louder human voice of past traumas from when we didn't feel like we had enough. A major way that we can experience this is with time, when we feel like: 1) we're too old for something, 2) we've missed the boat, or 3) we're about to miss the boat and step off the dock with an almightily embarrassing belly flop into the ocean. However, there are many people who achieve things later in life and there are many people who have spent decades getting to where they want to be.

While we're busy learning our lessons, many years can pass until we're finally ready to get going with our most purposeful work. This means that there are many examples of late bloomers who took the world by storm with a few grey hairs on their head and many, many rich years of experience behind them. McDonald's founder Ray Kroc opened his first restaurant in Des Plaines, Illinois, when he was 52. Also in the food business, Colonel Harland David Sanders was 62 years old when he started his first KFC franchise. Arianna Huffington founded *The Huffington Post* when she was 55. And Donald Fisher was 40 when he opened up the first ever Gap store in San Francisco, with no retail experience.[6]

Too often, people tell themselves all sorts of stories about their age and how much time they have left. There is always enough time if it's the right thing for you – regardless of your age in Earth years – so it's important not to let a limiting belief stop you pursuing what you really want. I've had clients in their 20s say that it's too late for them to start a podcast, add coaching to their business or grow their Instagram because the market is too saturated. However, what examples like those I've just shared in the previous paragraph show us is that we *do* have time to do the things we want to do. We just need to trust that our intuition is making us feel like certain things are meant for us because they are.

It's when we stress too much about the 'how' of making things happen that we become controlling, tugging and pulling at timelines to make them fit our own diary rather than the cosmic super-schedule that takes everything into account. If we feel like something is destined for us then it can't escape us, but what we can do in the meantime is think about all the previous topics we've covered.

What lessons have you learned? What are you ready to teach? And what can you enjoy now in your present moment? By focusing on all of these things you already have, you can settle into where you are, rather than rushing to what's next.

Are you having a towel moment?

When your mind is talking louder than your intuition and making you feel the fear, it's time to think of all the times when you've almost given up before a breakthrough. In spirituality, this can be referred to as the low tide before your wave comes in, or more commonly: a test. I don't think it is a test when we have to wait for things; however, there are so many times when I've felt like throwing in the towel before a breakthrough happened. I call this a 'towel moment'.

So, what do you do when you're having a towel moment? You think of all the times that you can look back on and be glad that you didn't give up, and you meditate if the mental chatter is getting too much. You give gratitude for where you are now and what you already have, and you practise putting a little more faith in yourself and the forces that be – knowing that it will all work out perfectly.

Having a moment to yourself when you feel overwhelmed is so important for you to be able to get grounded and see clearly what you need to do next. It's when you're silent that your intuition makes noise, so if you want to improve your intuitive ability, the way to do it is with a lot of meditation. If you can incorporate it into your daily routine, you'll find that you get more and more familiar with your own inner voice and how your intuition presents itself to you.

Intuition in action: meditation

Practising patience is a lot easier to do when you tune out of everything going on around you and align yourself fully with the present moment. Doing that will probably require you to leave your busy mind behind so that you can fully surrender to your soul and any information it wants to tell you.

If you're not familiar with meditating, there are many different ways to practise it and there's no right or wrong way – just whatever you're ready for and need in that particular moment. For example, sometimes when I'm really busy and can feel that my mind is getting out of control because stress is taking over, I'll set an alarm for two minutes on my phone in an attempt to empty my mind and re-centre. At other times, I'll do a 40-minute guided meditation and energy clearing with a big stick of selenite on my stomach. You can tailor your meditation practice to you, and ideally it will work best if it's regular; but as I've explained, whatever works for you in the present moment is okay.

If you're someone who struggles to tune out because you have mental chatter overload, start with a guided meditation (*see the link in the Resources section on page 205*) or by playing meditation music with binaural beats (you can find this free on YouTube). You might also find that it's easiest with no noise at all, in which case, sit in silence and practise a meditation such as this one:

✦ Sit comfortably or lie down with one hand on your heart and one hand on your stomach. Fully surrender to the present moment, bringing all of your awareness to the here and now – and out of any other times or places where your mind might still be.

✦ Imagine there's an invisible channel of energy going through the centre of your body, connecting you to the core of the Earth and going up as high as it can possibly reach into the Universe until it reaches a big ball of light. Imagine that the light is going through your body and tune in to how that would feel for you. This is how you get grounded and centred at the same time, and it only takes a minute to do this.

✦ Then, imagine that your mind is an empty white space with nothing at all in it. Just hold that space, and notice any thoughts that want to come through as though they're black words moving across that white space. This is how you can be the observer, reading your thoughts rather than giving in to them and taking them on.

✦ Hold the white space in your mind for as long as you can and notice if any feelings or intuitive guidance want to come through. You'll know if they're different from your thoughts because your thoughts are your everyday mental chatter, like what you're going to have for dinner, what's on your to-do list or where you need to go after your meditation. They are your thoughts, whereas any intuitive guidance might be answers to questions that you've asked before, directions on where to go next in life or a feeling of comfort telling you that everything's going to be okay because you're exactly where you need to be.

✦ You can either hold yourself in this meditation for as long as you like, or set an alarm if you're in between things that you need to do.

When you first start meditating, you might find that you fall asleep, which is relatively normal and not a bad thing. It just means that your body is grateful for the break and needs sleep more than anything else. If I'm struggling to sleep, I'll always do this practice of emptying my mind and holding the white space because it slows my body down and switches me over to my parasympathetic nervous system from my sympathetic nervous system (effectively telling my body that I'm moving from a state of do-ing to be-ing).

If this keeps happening and you want to stop it, try meditating sitting on a pillow with your back straight. A regular meditation practice will show you that you're not your thoughts. It will allow you to create space for your intuition to come through, and it will help you to recognize how your intuition is different from your everyday thoughts.

With a meditation practice, you'll be able to discern what intuition feels like for you, and it's the tool that's always going to bring you back to a place of patience. This is because when you're sitting in silence and your mind is empty, it can almost feel as though time stands still. And after a moment with nothing but yourself, you'll find that you're so much better equipped to keep going rather than giving in to any temporary ego-driven impulse. This isn't to say that all impulses are bad, because this is how creativity often comes in. The impulses create the idea, but it's committing to the cause that builds a masterpiece. The challenge is not to create, but to continue.

The wait is worth it

Rome wasn't built in a day, and the purposeful, aligned life that you've dreamed of probably won't be either. There may be many changes to be made, as well as many new things to learn. When people redirect their life towards a path that feels much more purposeful for them, it can often require years of training or starting at the bottom and working their way up. It could also mean saving for many years before they can invest in something they need, or even committing to something for the rest of their life, such as raising children (if their most purposeful and aligned mission is to be a parent).

When it's so obvious from examples like these that purposeful things in our life are built over time, why do we expect them to happen overnight? It might seem nice to take a shortcut, but really, it's the things we wait for and build that are usually the longest-lasting. I remember my grandfather saying to me that he wouldn't want to win the lottery because he found so much more satisfaction in the things he'd earned and accumulated over time. I always looked up to this and – now that I'm a bit older than I was when he said it to me – I can understand exactly what he means.

It's also really important to notice the things that you're *not* willing to wait for. The things that you don't want to be patient for and you really *do* want to throw in the towel over are also an intuitive sign, because perhaps giving up so readily means it's not truly what you want. The things we want with all of our heart and all of our soul, we'll keep in our heart until they're ready to arrive; so when we can shut the door on something and walk away from it, it's obviously not meant to be part of our future anymore. It's so important to notice how willing you are to sit in patience because it's an easy indicator of how deeply invested you are in something.

When you surrender to flow, let go and look out for the signs, opportunities will appear in ways that you didn't expect and on timelines that you could never have planned. My mother always used to say to me that 'God laughs at our plans' and now I know why. We don't have to control the things we love. We don't need to grasp in fear what is meant for us. And we don't have to worry when we know what we're meant for. Be patient in the pursuit of what you want. Time is a taskmaster we can all beat simply by be-ing.

Journalling questions to go deeper into Patience

🖊 What are you rushing towards because you're scared it might not happen?

🖊 What are you looking forward to without any expectation on the timeline?

🖊 What do you feel calm and certain about in your future?

Persevere

Question 18: What would you never give up on?

....

'Our greatest weakness lies in giving up. The most certain way to succeed is always to try just one more time.'

Thomas Edison

When you start following what feels in alignment, you'll find that something inside takes over and helps you to last so much longer than you used to. This longevity comes from a firm feeling that you know you're being guided to where you're meant to go, and it will allow you to persevere more easily. When you're moving down a path that you don't really want to be on, it makes it much more tempting to give up – so you're much more likely to. When you tune in to what you'd never give up on, you'll find that it's another clue to what's full of purpose and meaning for you.

Looking for where you have longevity

What will always pull you back from a towel moment is having some kind of certain intuitive sense that there's a reason for you not to throw in the towel. The road to anything worth having is probably going to have its own type of challenges, but when you commit to following your inspiration along the way, while surrendering to the moment you're in, you can focus on the path as it's unfolding in front of you and take each challenge as it comes. On the other hand, if you're feeling full of resistance about constantly having to overcome obstacles that you don't feel are worth facing, you're likely to cut your journey short.

It's by following what's important to you – as well as what you genuinely find fun and inspiring – that you'll get the gift of longevity. You'll find that you won't want time to pass, but it will anyway while you're busy doing what you love and living in the moment. Staying in something for a long time becomes so much easier when it's where you want to be, and it can completely eliminate the need for hustle, stress and resistance.

There's a very noticeable difference between what it feels like to persevere using hustle and force, as opposed to being able to persevere because you have an intuitive sense that you're being led to something worth carrying on for. When something is not a great fit for you, you might find that it's one obstacle after another and that the signs you receive are telling you to change track (if you're seeing any at all). You'll feel stressed and resistant in your body, and you'll constantly be plagued by thoughts of whether it's all worth it.

If you're on a path to something that's in tune with you, you might feel as though any challenges that come up are learning opportunities to help you on the rest of your journey. You'll have a sense of certainty that it's all going to work out somehow, even when it's not looking like it. You'll feel guided along and you'll trust in the timing of it all, because you'll have a calmness that comes from following what your intuition is telling you.

Now, this definitely isn't to say that discipline won't be required. Whatever you're wanting to pursue will probably require some discipline and resilience, but these qualities appear much more naturally when you're not having to really push something that isn't right for you. Longevity is staying in something you love because you love it, and you don't have to force yourself to be there. Perseverance is something that comes naturally when you know in your heart that you're in pursuit of your purpose.

'No' isn't always the final answer

There are endless examples that we can look up to if we feel like we're nearing a towel moment and we need some inspiration. Someone I really admire for their ability to persevere is Michael Jordan. He could have given up on playing basketball when he didn't get onto his varsity team in high school, and he could have started trying out for a different sport instead. But he'd never have known what career was on the other side of that 'no' if he hadn't persisted and tried again. A clue to his success is in his mindset and attitude to trying: 'I can accept failure; everyone fails at something. But I can't accept not trying.'[7]

When you know that what you're after is right for you, it'll give you a deep, burning sense that you absolutely cannot give up. You're much less likely to be knocked off your path by anyone or anything outside of you, including what anyone else says about whether it's possible for you or not. You'll simply know that you have to keep going because you'll feel certain that you can get there one day, whatever it takes.

Realizing what gives you this grit and resilience is incredibly empowering, so start to notice when you see your strongest self coming out. This tenacity to hold on could be coming from the fact that intuitively you just know you need to keep going. If you know something is right for you then it doesn't matter how many 'nos' you get. In some of the celebrity examples I've given in this book – such as Lady Gaga or Michael Jordan – they were told 'no' over and over and over again but they didn't listen... and look where they got to.

So, allow yourself to be guided by that innate, certain knowing that, once you're in tune with your intuition and where it's taking you, that takes absolute precedence over what anyone else says or thinks. As long as you're saying yes to you and your dreams, that's all that really matters because, eventually, you'll break your way through somehow if you can feel that it's destined to happen for you. Don't give up too soon if your intuition is telling you where you need to get to.

Intuition in action: breathwork

Breathwork is an incredible tool that can help you reduce anxiety, gain intuitive insights and connect back with your body. If you're feeling overwhelmed while you're persisting with something, breathwork is a great way to help you re-centre and ground yourself. At the end of breathwork sessions, I always find that I have incredible clarity and I'll get intuitive insights coming through about the names of courses that I need to offer next. This means that breathwork can be a great way to unlock any insights that you need to help you keep moving forwards.

It's possible to do guided breathwork sessions in person or online; however, you can also do it for free on your own, as follows:

+ After setting a timer on your phone for 45 minutes, play some calming music and lie down on your bed or sofa.

+ Put one hand on your heart and one hand on your stomach.

+ Breathe in as deeply as you can through your mouth, raising your belly and filling it up with air.

+ Then, before exhaling, take a second breath in and inflate your chest so that both your stomach and chest are fully inflated.

+ Exhale out fully through your mouth.

+ Create a rhythm for your inhale/inhale/exhale so they're all about equal in length.

+ After a few of these at a slower pace, once you're used to the rhythm, you can then take it faster.

You'll find that after about five minutes or so, your body might be telling you to stop. This is a perfect exercise in perseverance because, if you can keep going past that point, hopefully you'll find the benefits at the end to be worthwhile. Your body won't be used to getting so much oxygen, which is why your first reaction might be that you need to stop. If you're able to keep going – maybe with some breaks – throughout the 45-minute session, you might feel elated, have intuitive ideas coming through or even have an out-of-body experience. Overall, you might just feel more refreshed and rejuvenated.

Connecting with your breath will help you to feel more in tune with your body and regulate your own nervous system. It will prove that you can persevere and that the benefits will be there at the end when you do, if you know it's something that's right for you.

....

Your 'why' is your North Star

When you know what motivates you to keep going no matter what, you'll be able to see a much wider perspective of what needs to be done. You can think of this as your North Star. Being super clear on your North Star will allow you to keep moving towards it, regardless of how many times you have to adapt or overcome any issues that come up. This is because your 'why' will be so much bigger than anything temporary that's going on around you. Having a clear 'why' is really the key to having a purposeful life and by answering all of the questions in this book, you'll have a much better idea of what your North Star is and why you feel you're here on Earth.

Once you know your 'why', it becomes so much more important than how you're feeling in a particular moment. Any rejections or failures might shake you momentarily, but you'll eventually see how they can just be a clue for what you need to do better next time. This mindset is something that everyone can benefit from nurturing within themselves, but you'll see that it comes even more naturally when you're already invested in something on a soul level. Your 'why' is where you'll want to make the most impact, and you won't want to stop until you do.

Persevering into publishing

For me, perseverance looked like a three-year journey to finally get my first book published. I was so sure of what I wanted – to be a published author – but that didn't mean I knew how I was going to get there or how long it would take. Judging from the stories I'd heard about the J.K. Rowlings of the world, who'd had a more arduous time trying to get published than Harry did fighting off Lord Voldemort, I thought it might be a while. However, I was getting an incredible intuitive urge that I needed to persevere with one particular publisher, Hay House.

Now, this didn't make a lot of logical sense. Other people were telling me not to put all my eggs in one basket, and that I should maybe try some other publishers too. 'You'd probably have a better chance at a small local publisher,' a family member suggested sympathetically. My nail technician even told me that she used to work at a small publisher nearby, and while my logical mind recognized that it could be an opportunity to finally get my book printed and bound, my illogical, intuitive soul was still telling me that I was better off digging my heels in, waiting and doing whatever it took. I knew deeply where I wanted to be, and this is the kind of feeling you'll have that allows you to persevere again and again when you just *know* that something is right for you.

But – like the things you're willing to be patient for – it wasn't a desperate, grabbing feeling that it had to be *now*; I just knew that eventually it was going to be Hay House. That is, until I refreshed my inbox and the bold header of a new email appeared listing the winner and runner-up in a competition I'd applied for. No winner's phone call. No book contract. Gutted. I braced myself to try again and the timing of this second competition announcement was ideal: I'd be in Sorrento on the Monday after my wedding. *What an incredible way to celebrate!* I thought. *Being married on the Saturday, getting my dream book deal on the Monday. It could not get any better!*

My Italian-inspired dreams of becoming an author were crushed when I didn't win, again. I didn't know where to go from there, but I knew that I had to put it to the back of my mind because we were on holiday. The sun lit up the crystal-clear skies all day and the views were sublime – from the palm-tree-lined shopping streets filled with boutiques and pizzerias to the azure Mediterranean Sea that coloured the space between us and Mount Vesuvius on the opposite shore. There were ice-cream parlours with wooden swings hanging from the ceiling and limoncello was available on tap before, during and after every meal. Maybe I didn't win, but there was still a lot to celebrate.

It was another year, plus a few more months, before I finally received the email I'd been waiting for. Not only was there time between these three moments, but there were also three completely different book ideas and three completely new proposals. From the outside, you might say that it was just stubbornness or pride. But from the inside, I felt it was a deep inner knowing that this was exactly where my book was meant to be housed.

Keep going and continue on

Everyone is born with grit and resilience in them, including you. So, if you feel like you haven't tuned in to it yet, then maybe it's because you haven't been doing the right thing yet. The thing you really care about and want to keep going with. I promise you that, when you start following your intuition towards where it wants to take you, you'll be able to keep persevering through because you'll have a strong certainty about what's definitely meant for you.

The same is true when we're going after something that we know is going to have a big impact outside of our own lives. You might notice that you're much more willing to persevere when it's to do with another person or a greater cause. For example, parents are usually great at persevering when it comes to their children, and can keep going without much sleep through the tantrums and nappy changes because they feel it's worth it. If you can tune in to your source of strength, the one that makes you keep going forwards because you're guided and certain that it's worth the work, then you're tuning in to your place of power. However, if you're always feeling like you do genuinely want to give up, maybe your 'why' in what you're doing isn't strong enough. Not wanting to keep going can be a sign too.

Your purpose will probably require you to persevere sometimes. Not everyone who's achieved something great has done it overnight or found it easy. But there was something innate in their intuition telling them that they had potential and that they needed to keep going. This inner knowing will feed your mind with the motivation you need and when it comes through it's a sign that you have what it takes.

It's this deep, undeniable knowing that allows you to keep going even when the odds are stacked against you. Even with rejection after rejection after rejection, you can still continue on because part of you knows where you're going to get to eventually. You'll be able to move forwards without knowing the 'hows'. You'll try again in the face of the 'nos'. And you'll pick yourself up after every 'not yet'. Follow your feelings and keep going, no matter what. Giving up isn't an option when it's what you're meant to be doing.

Journalling questions to go deeper into Persevere

🖋 Can you think of a towel moment, when you almost gave up but didn't?

🖋 What motivates you to keep going, no matter what?

🖋 What is it that gets you through the tough times?

Perspective

Question 19: What are the greatest gifts you have in your life right now?

....

*'The play was a great success, but
the audience was a disaster.'*

Oscar Wilde

Recognizing what your greatest gifts are can give you a whole new perspective on life. To have a life at all is a gift, but it certainly doesn't always feel that way if you're living a life that's completely out of tune. We've already looked at what to purge from your life – what's in your life that you want to get rid of – but it's equally important to look at what you have in your life right now that feels like a blessing. Whether you see something as a blessing or not depends on your perspective. It's your perspective that creates the world you live in, in your own mind, which is why two people can see the same event completely differently.

Reality is subjective

How we see things really is what creates our reality, because reality is entirely subjective. They say that beauty is in the eye of the beholder, and that's because what looks good is based on how we're perceiving it through our own unique eyes. If you want to know more about how your perspective shapes your reality, there are plenty of fascinating YouTube videos by physicists describing the results of tests like the Double-Slit experiment and the Delayed-Choice Quantum Eraser experiment, which show how the physical universe is affected by our consciousness. I'm no quantum physicist, so I don't plan on going into this in any more detail here, but I definitely recommend diving deeper into this topic because it proves how important our perspective is in directing probable wave forms to create our tangible reality.

What we direct our consciousness towards gives it life. This is where the saying comes from: what we focus on grows. We give momentum to the things we direct our consciousness towards, so we would be wise to ensure that we're using the power of our perspective with the respect it deserves. You literally have the power to define all of your experiences from the past, present and future. How you experience your own life isn't up to anyone but you, because you're the director of your own consciousness and you're the one with an intuition telling you what feels good, bad, off, exciting or right for you.

The enormous role that consciousness plays in our life isn't yet known by most people. But thankfully, there are people in the scientific community supporting what the spiritual community has said all along: that your thoughts really do create your reality. Whatever lens you choose to see through (the spiritual or the scientific), the most important thing to take away is the life-changing power of your perspective. If you focus on what you want to see more of, then that's going to expand and take up space in your awareness; whereas if you focus on the things that feel bad to you, then your experience of them will only get worse.

Another way that this happens is through our Reticular Activating System, or RAS. Our RAS is a system in our brain that tells us what is and isn't worth focusing on, which is why we can notice things around us so much more once we direct our attention onto them. When I was planning to move to Australia at one point in my life, I kept noticing all of the things around me that bore an emblem of the 'land down under'. My microphone had been made there, as well as a birthday card that I was writing for a friend, and a tote bag hung in a shop window with a beautiful floral pattern across the front. My eyes zoomed in on the word at the bottom below the teal printed leaves: Australia.

We can use this to our advantage by focusing on the gifts we have in our life, which will allow us to perceive more gifts unwrapping around us in our own world. The things we might want to focus on in our life could be the enormous amount of love we have for our children, the smell of fresh coffee in the morning or a run in the park on a crisp autumn evening. Giving gratitude for the sweet moments that could be viewed as mundane is what grows them into a gift. When we love our life, we'll soon have more to love. Being grateful is what turns our focus towards all the ways that the Universe has been generous to us – as well as the ways that we've shown love for ourselves by creating something perfectly in tune.

Turn your attention to what's already in tune

By noticing the greatest gifts in your life right now, you can turn your attention to what's already in tune, so you know what you're looking for more of in your future. Awareness of what you want will tune you in to each opportunity when it comes up so that you'll know whether it's a good or bad one for you. What's in tune may choose you, in those times when a fateful whirlwind happens that whips your world into a frenzy before landing you in the middle of the life you always wanted. But, for most of the time, you'll need to be making each decision from an empowered place of knowing what you *do* and *don't* want in your life. What you want more of you can have more of, so it's important to become crystal-clear about what you truly treasure in your space, schedule and social life.

Intuition in action: gratitude practice

Writing a gratitude list is super simple and it's how you can remind yourself of everything great going on in your life. This is an exercise you can do every day or a few times a week, but the more you do it, the more benefits you'll have. Research has found that we can improve our long-term happiness by more than 10 per cent simply by journalling for five minutes every day about what we're grateful for.[8] On some days this exercise will feel easy and other days it'll feel harder, but whatever is going on in your life, if you can always do this exercise then you'll realize there are plenty of things to be grateful for.

To write your gratitude list, grab your journal and choose one of these sentence-starters:

✦ 'I am grateful for...'

✦ 'I am very thankful for...'

✦ 'My heart is full of gratitude today because...'

Then, simply write the option you've chosen over and over again and complete the sentences with each individual thing you feel grateful for that day. Include the big things and the small things, whether it's being alive for another day, a dinner you enjoyed or being able to see nature from your window. You can write down people, places, possessions or activities you've enjoyed. The most important thing is to feel the gratitude as you're writing them down.

Knowing with certainty what the greatest gifts in your life are reminds you of what it feels like when something is totally in tune with you and making your soul sing. It also makes it clearer what doesn't, because you'll know when there's the absence of this feeling. You can prove that it *is* possible to align yourself with things that feel pleasing to your intuition by seeing how you have done so already.

Feeling good about what you have isn't necessarily some far-away feeling – it's something you can have now, which just needs to be found in the busy life that you're living. It's like leaning in to smell the roses, without letting life pull you away. What you elect to keep on this journey of living in tune can be only things that serve a greater good for you, and when you consistently write a gratitude list you may find more of them in the days that you're living now than you realized. There is no reason for you to deny your intuition by being without the things that you want – you just need to know what they are, and notice how many of them you already have.

When we feel like something is missing from our life, sometimes it's only a new perspective that's required. Other things in our busy daily lives can cloud our perspective because we get so distracted that we don't even notice what feels fantastic anymore. So, by taking some time in the morning (or the evening) to get into a habit of writing this gratitude list repeatedly to see what appears, it'll become very clear what we hold close as the greatest gifts in our life. Again, this list is going to be different for everyone. Some people will absolutely adore the moments that they've had alone to themselves, whereas other people will be grateful for the times when they could immerse themselves in the energy of other people. It's not for us to judge ourselves based on what we find, but rather, to realize and accept ourselves and our desires.

It's also important to note that this isn't an analytical decision; it's an exercise in noticing what feels good for us. Sometimes, analytical decisions can't save us, because it's when we think we 'should' want something that we can trap ourselves in our own misguided logic. When we know ourselves, we're able to use our intuition instead. A lot of us have ended up in lives that are out of tune because we lost touch with our intuition as a result of the modern Western world not valuing this extra-sensory intelligence we all have. And yet this is exactly what it is: the highest form of intelligence we have available to us on a personal level. We just need to be clear on what our own perspective is rather than being tricked into seeing through anyone else's, or through the perspective of what we 'should' want more of.

Your gifts can guide you

Instead, we can know that those who are tuned in are the wise ones. We all have the chance to tune in, listen to our intuition and be guided to what feels good and right for us, instead of walking into the things that will make us feel lost and alone. When something you currently have in your life makes you feel complete, whole, joyous and blissed-out, that's exactly what you'll want to get hold of. These will be things that are perfectly in tune with you and your purpose, and they're the things that your internal navigation system is driving you towards.

You have them in your life now because you were guided towards them at one point, so equally, you can figure out what's next by remembering how you tuned in to them before you got them. It's not just the physical items that will feel like a gift – it's also the activities in your life that you love. If your work feels like a gift then you're one of the lucky ones! And if it doesn't yet, you can fix it so it does. If you love doing card readings, then maybe you can start a side-hustle that could one day turn into a magical divination business. If cooking and hosting dinner parties for your friends is joyous for you, then who's to say that couldn't turn into a weekend – and soon to be full-time – catering business?

I realized that writing was a gift for me long before I ever was paid for it. It felt good back when I was writing Instagram quotes and collecting words that meant my Notes app took up a disproportionate amount of storage on my phone, but I had absolutely no idea how I'd be able to expand on that. Obviously, I wanted this thing that felt good to take up more space in my life, and even though I didn't know *how*, I knew I was starting to get a clear perspective on how work could become a gift instead of a curse. For way too many years, I'd been moving from one thing to another trying to find what I'd enjoy doing enough to actually want to do it all day every day. Money? No. Fashion? Nope. Making coffee? Definitely not.

Yet we know by now from what we've covered in previous chapters that these things were great gifts on my journey too, because they helped to shape my perspective. They made it clearer for me to see what felt like a gift by helping me to know what definitely did not. As I focused in on writing spiritual musings and devoted more time to it during early mornings, evenings and weekends, I could see more clearly that this was something that lit a spark in me. I started to dream and wonder what it would be like to spend more of my days writing, losing track of time instead of wishing that every minute would pass by sooner.

Once you're able to get a glimpse of your purpose by seeing what you want more of in your life, you can expand on any of the wonderful things you've already tuned in to. You can grow your gifts into ever more present and powerful parts of your life. Your perspective of what's going to be great for you and your life is unique, and it's important to define it so that you can work towards living the life that's a perfect fit *for you*. Your perspective really does shape your reality, so beware of where you direct your consciousness and make sure that you're sending it towards all the things you can easily give gratitude for. Through being able to see what the greatest gifts in your life are, you'll be able to see yourself more clearly.

Journalling questions to go deeper into Perspective

🖉 What can't you live without?

🖉 What do you look forward to most every day?

🖉 Is there anything you'd multiply in your life, if you could?

Prosper

Question 20: What do you need to feel truly prosperous?

. . . .

'Possession of material riches, without inner peace,
is like dying of thirst while bathing in a lake.'

Paramahansa Yogananda

Prosperity, like perspective, is totally subjective. Abundance is a universal feeling with different routes to reaching it, so you need to find your path there in a way that feels aligned for you. Chasing a definition of abundance that's not going to really fulfil you will drain your energy, and more importantly, your time. By choosing to do more of what makes you feel prosperous, you will automatically unlock new avenues of abundance as you follow the feeling rather than the final result. Endless excess is available to you in the form of a feeling if you're open to experiencing the great richness of life in your own way.

What does prosperity mean to you?

Wealth is a wonderful thing to have, but it's only worthwhile if it's part of a life that is being lived in tune. I don't think anyone will be surprised to hear that an out of tune life is often the result of chasing money alone, without taking into account the parts of our purpose that will actually make us feel whole and fulfilled. If we're not teaching what we know, sharing the solutions we think will help the world, following our inspiration or any of the other things we've covered in the previous chapters, we could end up with a bank account full of cash and a heart that feels empty.

In no way is this to say that financial wealth isn't important or that we shouldn't be aiming for it! It's just absolutely imperative to understand your own priorities when it comes to what prosperity *actually* means to you. Otherwise, you could fall into the trap of thinking that money is what you want most, only to find that once you get it, there's still something deeply wrong because it hasn't given you the feeling you thought it would. By chasing the wrong things, you will never win the race. Only by being aware of and aligned with what you truly want can you feel abundant, rich and wealthy in all of the ways that will bring meaning to your life.

The worst thing about pursuing prosperity in the wrong way is the feeling of wasted time. If you're not spending your time in a way that feels right for you, no amount of money can cure that. When I used to sit in a grey swivel desk chair all day, looking after the accounts of 'Top 50' high net-worth commercial clients – big companies that everyone knows and is probably a customer of – it was a huge novelty at first. I felt like I'd be prepared to do anything for the amount of money I was earning because it was the most I'd ever been paid.

Then, over time, the money became less and less valuable to me. It's importance to me shrank further and further until my need for purpose consumed it in one hungry bite. I still love the idea of luxurious material things, but there was a price that I wasn't willing to pay, and that price was my time. Just being able to buy things alone wasn't ever going to make me feel prosperous if I felt like my soul was suffering for it every day. The moment when I realized that something had to change was while I was on a flight to Rome reading an issue of *Cosmopolitan*.

Revelations in Rome

This was a few years PSA (pre-spiritual awakening), so don't judge me for my taste in holiday reading material. Three girls I'd lived with at university were sitting in the plane seats next to me on a Ryanair flight from London to begin a long weekend away. I literally lived for these moments. Any moment I was free from the office was great, but being able to leave the country was even better. With our cabin-sized suitcases squeezed under the seats in front of us, we had four days of vacation fun ahead – Italian style! Pizza in the Piazza Navona, posing for pictures on the Spanish Steps, a guided walking tour around the Vatican and, of course, the Colosseum.

However, at the start of any weekend there'd always be a knot in my stomach, which would tighten and squeeze whenever the thought of what was to come on Monday crossed my mind. I knew I was incredibly lucky to have my job, and I'd worked hard for years to get there, but that only added to my confusion. I didn't entirely know what I was feeling, but it didn't feel good. If I sensed my soul tugging at the stomach knot, I'd try to turn my attention back to the fun that lay immediately ahead and whatever I was enjoying in that moment. That said, I knew what wish I'd be making when I threw a coin in the Trevi Fountain later that weekend.

As I tried to switch on holiday mode in my head, I flicked through the pages of *Cosmo*. I definitely wasn't looking for answers there, but I found something that I thought might be one: an article about a day in the life of a fashion buyer. This woman was flying business class to Tokyo, Milan and New York, and putting designer handbags on her company credit card in the name of research. The bit that will always stick with me was when she was asked what the worst part of her job was, to which she replied: 'Being in a buyers' meeting when I'm tired after a trip to Tokyo.' *Some negative*, I thought. *I want in!*

When I read that article, it was like the little me that lives inside my head pulled a cord and clicked on a ceiling light that lit everything up. For the first time, I was seeing what I was missing, right there on the glossy page in front of me. As you know, I did transition to fashion and that wasn't right for me either, but at that point I'd never even considered that I could do work for any reason other than money. I'd always done jobs because I *had to* in order to have money, so if I *had to* then I might as well justify it by making as much money as I possibly could. I thought that was the only sane way to justify my suffering in any job – by having something concrete to show for it.

But what the article revealed to me was that people actually had fun at work; that making money could come from a job that you enjoyed and that there were options available other than being a slave to the silver sterling. What I was being led to wasn't directly my purpose, but it was the next unmissable step on the route leading to it. All I needed was an example to show that it was possible; someone to prove that different ways of attaining prosperity were available.

If you can find some expanders to strengthen your belief that it's possible to find prosperity in an aligned and enjoyable way, then that will help you to trust that it's possible for you too.

Abundance attracts abundance

If you believe that you can live a prosperous life in the way that feels right for you, then you'll find that you start being guided towards it. Your eyes need to be open to see the signs, and your mind needs to be paying attention to what your gut is telling you. Once you know what you want and need in order to live a life that feels abundant, you can start finding ways to make it happen. But you *must* be aware of what you need and want first. It's not being aware of what will make us feel prosperous that causes us to burn out quickly while still feeling like something is missing on the inside.

Your intention is powerful, so just noticing what doesn't feel right and what isn't making you feel prosperous is the initial catalyst you need to start looking for alternative options. The time I spent in that office chair, crossing off the days with dwindling motivation to keep working, was the catalyst I needed to keep looking for my purpose. In my opinion, it's worse to keep living a life that's comfortably uncomfortable because the catalyst never comes and a feeling of true prosperity may never be found.

When you're trying to do the best you can to honour your purpose, rather than just doing things because you feel you *have to* in order to get money, the outcome completely changes. You attract amazing friends, clients and opportunities. And needless to say, the impact you'll have on them is far greater when you're actually emotionally invested in your work – instead of just waiting until the end of the day for it to be over. The clients who choose to work with me all have this same goal in common: they truly want to heal and uplift the world because they've recognized that they have some special gift or passion that will enable them to do that. Once they've realized what that special gift or passion is, it gets harder and harder to deny it.

When I start working with a new client who wants to start their own spiritual business, it's usually because they've reached the same point I'd got to, once I felt I'd got as far as I could in a traditional full-time job. It's because they know that their purpose lies somewhere within spirituality, whether it's healing, teaching spiritual concepts, writing spiritual books or giving readings. The type of clients I've attracted over the years has really made me believe that we attract the exact people we're meant to work with, and this is something that only happens once we're fully aligned with our purpose and sharing our authentic message.

My clients also have in common a genuine desire to help, and it's that feeling of fulfilling their purpose and serving the world in whatever way they uniquely do – whether it's card readings, birth chart readings, Human Design, Reiki, quantum healing, coaching or writing – that makes them feel abundant. And as a result, they get financial prosperity in return.

In the same way that having only financial prosperity without inner abundance will make you feel like something is missing, the reverse can also be true. I've come across people who don't feel like they're making anywhere near enough money. This can mean that they're having to hold onto a full-time job that they don't like to make ends meet, while running themselves into the ground on evenings and weekends. It can mean that they feel disheartened and put off from pursuing their purpose because they don't have the financial prosperity they need to support them, so they feel like they're failing.

In some cases, I've seen people have to give up their spiritual business altogether because they weren't able to make it financially viable, and then return to their old job. This is always incredibly sad to see, so I also want to emphasize that feelings of abundance and financial prosperity go hand in hand with each other. Don't ever feel bad about wanting a flourishing financial situation in your life either, as it will keep you in the work you love and allow you to bring your best energy to what you're doing every day.

Intuition in action: the 'me' you want to be

Once you have a better idea of what feels good to you, it should start to become clear what your ultimate end goal is: how you want to feel every day; the people and things you want to be surrounded by; and the way you want to spend your time. If you were totally in tune with your intuition, and money was no object, it's likely that some things in your life would change. When money isn't something that you have to think about, you have total freedom to live your life exactly how you want to, without having to sacrifice anything due to material constraints.

Therefore, an exercise that will help you to uncover what your intuition really wants you to do is to imagine that you have all the money your heart desires. This amount will be different for everyone, but – however much money you think you'd need to be totally free financially – insert this number into the following sentence, 'The £X version of me', and write it down at the top of a page in your journal. Then, step into the mindset and feeling of being the person who literally has this amount of money in their bank account. Tune in to how you feel and answer the following questions to reveal what you really want and what makes you feel prosperous aside from money.

As the £X version of you:

+ How would you spend most of your time?

+ How would you feel different emotionally?

+ How would you make better decisions for your health and body?

+ What would you value most in your life?

+ What would you prioritize? And how is it different from what you're prioritizing today?

Imagining that money is out of the equation will give you total freedom to explore your intuition. By being unhindered, you can flow freely as the version of you with no restrictions on what you can do with your time. You already know how you want to live but you might be holding back because you think it's not possible without having enough money.

However, by doing this exercise, you'll see that in your heart you know what you'd most like to do because it's full of purpose and fun for you, rather than it being something you feel like you *have* to do. When you set your intuition free from the constraints of daily life, even if it's only in your mind for a moment during this exercise, you'll see that you have an acute awareness of what your intuition is pulling you towards. It can show you how to feel prosperous in how you're spending your time and who you're being.

Working with people who all want so much more than money alone has given me a huge amount of hope. Seeing people who want to give so much and genuinely heal the world is a beautiful thing, and simply by working with them I feel more prosperous and abundant. So many people hold on to unhappy lives because they don't want to give happiness to anyone else, but those who truly want to prosper will know that they thrive best when they want everyone else to thrive too.

We can all rise together and we can all prosper at the same time. It's not a zero-sum game, and there's space for us to live the life that we feel will make us the most abundant on both the inside and the outside. Having our material needs met will make our life so much easier, of course, but it's important that chasing the coin alone doesn't come at a tremendous cost: the detriment of our soul. Poverty can be felt on the inside and on the outside, but when we're clear on our intention about what we want abundance to feel like, we can start moving our life in the direction of our desires.

Journalling questions to go deeper into Prosper

What does abundance mean to you?

What is more important to you than money?

In what different ways do you want to be repaid when you invest your time in something?

Purpose

Question 21: What is the quiet calling of your soul saying to you now?

....

'Because success without purpose
is a pretty meaningless life.'

Zac Efron

By now, hopefully you'll see that there are ways for you to embody all the things we've covered in the previous chapters. By knowing the answers to these 21 questions, your soul is giving you the clues to what your purpose is. It's so important to know how you can connect to purpose because that's how you can feel whole, aligned and free – and when you're feeling free, as the full version of you, that's when magic will start to flow into your life.

Your purpose is something only you can tune in to. Your freedom will be found by following your own self-defined path, and your feelings are the only thing that can lead you to the truth of what is really right for you. When you listen to your soul and recognize your intuition as the superpower that it is, the world can become yours in whatever way you want it to be. The best type of success that will never burn out is the one that is fuelled by purpose.

Step into your light

As a human, you come here with so many gifts and you have a unique ability to change the world in some way. However, only by seeing this truth and being confident in it can you start to step into your light. This is where so many people fall short and why so many people never live in tune with their purpose; because they don't believe that it's possible for them and they haven't seen enough examples of purpose-full people to inspire them. This is the first reason it's so important for you to be enjoying an intuitively led life of purpose – so that other people can see how you're glowing and what impact you're having, to prove to them that it can be their reality too.

Another reason it's so important for you to bring purpose into your life is so that you can see and accept all the beautiful opportunities that life has to offer you. So many doors get unlocked when you tune in to your purpose because it's the magic key to having a clear flow of abundance into your life. When you're resisting the work you're doing, or the relationship you're in, or how you're spending your time, you're blocking off some of that abundance. You stay stuck in a state of frustration and contraction, focusing on the negatives rather than the positives. It's harder to be grateful in this state and it's harder to see all the joy that's available to you because you're not choosing joy for yourself.

The next reason it's imperative for you to find your purpose is because it's what you're *meant* for. It's literally what you're here to do and it's what you'll be the very best at doing. If you've found that you've spent your life so far feeling like you never really excelled at anything and you don't quite know what you're here for, then you haven't found it yet. And that's okay, but please know that it's definitely out there and that a life full of purpose is your birthright.

The Universe will support you in your purpose

It's very rare for someone to live their entire life in tune and it usually requires passing through the process outlined in this book – such as going through pain and learning certain lessons – for it to be revealed. Divine timing is a very important piece of connecting with your purpose, because these other things will have to happen first for you to realize what that purpose is. So until then, what's the most important thing for you to do right now? It's to open up to the possibility of being completely in tune with your purpose. Then you can start aligning with the highest possible life you're destined for, because you're making that commitment to change. Have a strong intention that you're being led to your purpose now and tune in to the feeling of being ready to embody it.

This is a really helpful exercise to do because it will reveal any resistance you have around why it's not possible for you to live in your purpose, as well as any fears you have around making changes in your life. If you're not in tune with your purpose yet, some changes will be required for you to get there. Noticing the resistance and fears you have, around making changes and around getting out of situations that you know *definitely* aren't aligned with joy and meaning, will be a pivotal step towards you making space for something better to enter your life instead. Setting this clear intention that you're ready for your purpose, and genuinely being open to receive it, will activate your intuition to start feeling for clues, while signalling to the Universe that you're ready to start receiving signs.

When you're ready to make the leap, the Universe will be ready to catch you. Being afraid to let go and make space is what usually stops people surrendering to where they're really meant to be. Like a river that moves through to wash away the old, letting go will also invite in the new. I found this when I got offered that well-paid part-time lecturing job out of the blue, three months after walking away from office life for the last time. This isn't possible for everyone, but it was what a leap of faith looked like for me at the time, and then it wasn't long before I was handed the perfect paid opportunity to support me while I built my dreams. It also allowed me to practise overcoming one of the hurdles still in the way of me being able to live out my purpose as a spiritual author, coach and teacher: a fear of public speaking.

Again, this shows the importance of divine timing, because you only get what you're ready for. This means that you need to have sharpened the tools in your toolkit enough to be able to perform your purpose. Another thing you'll notice is that I've listed multiple things here as parts of my purpose. You'll probably find that there are a few different activities that feel aligned for you. Embrace all of you, in your multidimensional glory, so that you can receive everything you truly want to receive.

You don't have to say no to any part of yourself that is real. You can embrace any duality you find because your idiosyncrasies exist for a reason, and they will attract you to the perfect people and opportunities. By accepting all of yourself and the different parts of your purpose, you'll also inspire others and show them that you don't need to confine yourself to one particular box. If you add judgement into the mix, it's going to close your mind down instead of keeping it open and receptive to whatever the Universe wants to bring you next, once the time is right.

Impact beyond the individual

This is the thing about purpose: it's meant to weave into the world in some way that will have an impact reaching further than just you. Your impact is meant to be seen, shared, enjoyed and celebrated beyond the confines of your own mind. Therefore, another way that you can know if something is your purpose is by the positive impact you see it having. Of course, it has to feel good for you on the inside too (otherwise, it's not your purpose), but when the joy you feel spreads out to others, that's a sure sign of being aligned because the universal life force that connects all of us is flowing freely through you.

When life is flowing freely, it becomes easy and – in my opinion – being in your purpose is the easiest place to be because your soul feels settled and at peace. When you don't feel like you're doing what you're meant to be doing, any symptoms of an unsettled soul are your warning signs, telling you that more tuning in is needed to keep moving forwards to what your soul wants. Then, once you're living your purpose, you'll appreciate every day lived in tune even more because you've had the chance to experience what life is like when you're out of tune.

If you find yourself in that position, where you feel like your soul is unsettled and you're in the shadow side of that contrast, then evaluating what is and isn't working for you right now – using all the questions provided in this book – is what will help you to see clearly. By leaning into the life that you already have, you can feel for what's aligned for you and what you should keep following going forwards. As I mentioned at the very beginning, when you first started reading this book, it's important not to distract yourself, so that you can feel where any unsettled itch is coming from. Turning away will never reveal to you what you're meant to see. By seeing the truth of who you are and what you want, you can accept what you really need and start walking your own unique path towards it.

Not a client case study: stocks and bonds to legally blonde

My best friend Becca was the perfect example for this case study, even though she's never been a client of mine. It seemed like from the moment our eyes met across the classroom in Year 2, she was always set on being a lawyer. However, back then I also wanted to be a vet – and for both of us, things changed along the way. As we stayed friends throughout school, our paths diverted from our original plans and we both went down the economics route instead. This led her into a long and successful career as an investment manager in London.

However, while her salary was rising each year as she progressed, she still knew she was made for more. Then, as her Saturn return drew near, it was her time to move back into alignment, making her leave her London career behind to move closer to what she felt was her calling. Her biggest passion had always been issues of justice and human rights, and her love of words aligned easily with a legal career. After saving for a year, she got a place on a law conversion course and decided to study something that really gave her a sense of purpose.

As I've explained before, deciding to align with a more purposeful life isn't necessarily going to happen overnight. It might require saving, changing, making space and removing everything that isn't it; but it'll be worth it in the end when you feel like you're in a life that you're meant for, and you don't have to force yourself to be someone you're not. There is always a space for you to be who you are. Honour what you truly want because your biggest purpose of all is to be the most accurate and easy expression of you.

Stop settling and set your sights high

It's time for you to stop settling for anything less than aligned because a sense of purpose is always possible. It's important to know what your purpose is because by living it you'll impact so many more people than just you. Your soul is calling you quietly towards the place where it will feel at peace, so it's your job to tune in and listen to what it has to say. This can be scary, but you'll know when you're ready to take the leap; and when you do, the Universe will be waiting.

Every lesson you've learned up to this point has been useful somehow – whether it was a fun one or a painful one – so honour any contrast that you've experienced, because that has also been guiding you towards your purpose by helping you to know what you need to walk away from. Remember that you're multifaceted and try not to narrow your vision of what your purpose 'should' be, as you may find it in a few different areas that somehow weave into one another. Once you know what you're here for, you can finally make your mark on the world and enjoy the feeling of *Living in Tune*.

Journalling questions to go deeper into Purpose

🖋 What lights you up more than anything else?

🖋 When do you feel most free, powerful and authentically yourself?

🖋 What gift can you bring to the world?

Conclusion

....

'You have to leave the city of your comfort
and go into the wilderness of your intuition...
what you'll discover will be wonderful.
What you'll discover will be yourself.'

Alan Alda

Your intuition is your inner guide to everything you desire. What you love can lead you forwards when you trust how you feel and are guided by that more than anything else. Putting logic above love doesn't work best when it comes to matters of the heart and soul, which see through a spiritual lens rather than a practical one. As humans, we're tasked with keeping the practical matters in mind to survive, but it's our soul's assignment to ensure that we find a way to integrate a sense of purpose too.

Keep flowing with your inner knowing

Living in tune feels like flowing with your inner knowing. It looks like a life that you've chosen and it's how you can be the best version of you. Being in tune is the easiest way to live once you're there, but it doesn't mean that getting there is going to be easy. It will require making adjustments and fully accepting where you are right now, with all that doesn't feel like it belongs yet. There are going to be times in your life and situations where it's not possible for you to get in tune, for reasons out of your control, but it's what you can always aim for – and when you set that intention and decide that you're going to make a change, you'll start noticing new solutions and new opportunities.

Being in alignment is the optimal state for your energy and for your soul. It's where the magic happens. It's where manifestations flow in. It's where you flow. It's where inspiration enters and where you can create incredible magic in the world. But when that happens, things that don't fit anymore just don't fit. They might fall out and they might float away, but I want you to consider this as an energetic detox. They're detoxing out of your life because they've served their purpose and they've done their time. When you create space and time in your life to just flow and be, you'll find that the right words, opportunities, messages and people might cross your path. Space is a sacred symbol of trust, and by keeping it, you're making a commitment to fill it only with something that's worthy.

Listening to your intuition is how you get in tune. When you feel in tune and you're honouring your inner knowing, you'll naturally slip into a more purposeful life. You'll feel like you're doing the things you're meant to be doing because you can't see anything else you think would fit better. Life has more meaning once days become something you want to stay in, rather than watching the clock until it's time to get out of them. If a sense of purpose is what's missing, then the most important thing is to start putting your own feelings first, because they're always trying to lead you to the outcomes you really want.

The intuitive mind is not the logical mind, so they may say different things. This is why so many people put their intuition on the back burner and live a life ignoring it, not understanding why they feel so out of tune. The logical mind wants to take care of us and keep us alive, but thoughts are like waves on the ocean of the mind and they can rise up and retreat at any moment without warning. With their louder voice and our lack of listening, our logical thoughts will often consume our intuitive feelings, like a tidal wave swallowing a life raft. But by finding a way to balance our intuitive mind and our logical mind, we'll find a sense of peace and balance for all parts of us to flow and perform their perfect function.

When you start listening to your intuition and honouring it as the gift that it is, you can find your unique path and start listening to your own voice above anyone else's. It only takes not listening to it a few times to realize the intense ache that it can leave in your heart when you're going against what you know is really right for you. Starting to listen to your intuition is another choice you make, and it means pausing before every decision to quiet your mind and feel how you actually want to go forwards. Rather than planning it out or thinking about it too much – because your thoughts are often filled with fears about what you 'should' be doing – by sensing what will make you feel either more free or more weighed-down, you can get a clear intuitive sense of what your future will be like. You can be your own oracle because you don't need anyone else to give you the answers that you already know within.

Keep following the signs and synchronicities

When things don't feel right, it's a sign just as much as when things do. That uneasy feeling in your gut telling you that you need to leave something behind is your intuition speaking to you through your body. The same is true for a sense of dread, a heaviness on your shoulders or being unable to sleep because you know that something is wrong. Your body is a tool, so you can use it to give you the answers you need. When you don't listen to your intuition, it will get louder and louder until it forces you to notice what you need to see. The Universe may also support this process with signs or events that make you change path, so in my opinion it's the easier option to listen to your intuition first, take note, and move accordingly, before the decision leaves your control and an unexpected change shakes you free.

Signs will also appear to tell you when you're going in a favourable direction. White feathers might fall from the sky in front of you or you might get repeating numbers or spooky synchronicities that tie in perfectly with what you were thinking at that exact moment. When you feel like everything seems to be supporting your intuitive inkling in a way that you can't quite explain, that's worth noticing too. External signs of support can validate your intuition and strengthen your belief in yourself to make the changes that you need to make. When this starts to happen, it feels like you can relax into life and let it hold you and support you. Let it cradle you with divinely timed synchronicities along your search for purpose. Lean into its arms and see where it wants to carry you next.

I had one of these synchronicities that spoke to my soul when I realized with my intuition that I was going to get published by Hay House. When I went to the Writer's Workshop for the first time in 2018, it was a huge turning point for me. Until that fateful weekend, I'd naively thought that you just needed to be a good writer to be offered a book deal, get published and take your rightful place at the top of the *New York Times* bestsellers list. How wrong I was! Yet from the Instagram posts that were doing well and the blog that I was loving writing, a deeper urge was telling me that I could write something much longer, which would one day be printed, bound and put into people's homes. For the next two years, this was my biggest goal and my biggest focus. As well as writing my blog and building my Instagram following, I continued being a voracious reader and an avid student of every online course I could find.

One day, when I was sitting with a Wayne Dyer book next to me, I was thumbing through the pages quickly, as if it was a flipbook about to reveal an animated cartoon character running across the page and doing something funny, until the book fell open on one of the pages at the back. I found myself staring at it, thinking *Why on Earth am I looking at a back page?* However, as my eyes focused and my attention went from inside my head to the page in front of it, I realized what was written in huge letters: JOIN THE HAY HOUSE FAMILY.

As I stared at it, I felt like it was speaking to just me. If you've had one of those moments when you feel like you've noticed an important signpost from the Universe, you know what it feels like. On paper, for someone else reading it, it might not seem significant at all – or little more than a coincidence – but I had that moment when it was as though my hair was being blown off my face by a chorus of singing angels that had materialized off the page. It felt like the Universe was giving me an instruction, so from that point on, I didn't apply anywhere else. I knew where I had to be, and it was Hay House or nothing.

When things aren't really right, you have to control them to hold everything together. But when you're aligned and in tune with what you're meant to be doing, you don't have to worry about things falling apart. In fact, you'll find that everything will conspire to keep you in your right place. Magical moments of synchronicity and the people you need will mysteriously appear on your path, just when you need them, and no later than when you feel like it's almost time to give up. The support that slips into the burgeoning cracks when you're about to falter is the same invisible force that's always sending you signs, messages and feelings: the invisible essence of you that's an indivisible part of the Universe.

Keep living in tune

By knowing the answers to these 21 questions, you know yourself better than a lot of people do. It's my mission through my work to connect everyone back with their spirituality so that they can feel a strong sense of self and live the most fulfilling life possible. The *Living in Tune* framework can be applied to individual areas of your life, and I wholeheartedly encourage using your intuition as your secret source of success when you're an entrepreneur. For more information about my services, as well as free blogs and podcasts, you can go to www.LizRoberta.com.

If you enjoyed this book, share a picture of the cover on Instagram and tag me (@iamLizRoberta) so that I can share it on my page. Whether it's with a coffee, on the beach or on a trip somewhere special, I'd love to know where you were reading it and what your favourite parts were. If you know someone you feel would benefit from what's inside this book then please pass it on, because we can all find life a little bit easier when we're living in tune.

Honour and trust your feelings as the divine signposts they are because everything weaves together in sacred serendipity to reveal your destiny and light the way with what you love. If you open your eyes to what you've already learned, you have a chance to see the intricate design that always exists. What if there are no accidents in life, including the birth of yours? Who could you be if you decided to live in tune with yourself, and with life itself? Be earnest in the pursuit of your life's work as a human with purpose and passions. This is your life, and to not live it is a waste.

Resources

For your free 'Tune Out & Tune In' meditation and printable Living in Tune workbook, go to:

www.LizRoberta.com/LivinginTune

On Instagram: @iamLizRoberta

On Facebook: @iamLizRoberta

For the podcast, find 'The Spiritual Success Podcast with Liz Roberta' on Apple Podcasts, Spotify or anywhere else you listen to podcasts

For the blog, go to:

www.LizRoberta.com/TheBlog

To see what trainings and programmes are currently running, go to:

www.LizRoberta.com

References

1. Maslow, A.H. (1943), 'A Theory of Human Motivation', *Psychological Review*, 50 (4): 370–396. DOI: 10.1037/h0054346

2. Root-Bernstein, R. and Root-Bernstein, M. (2010) 'Einstein on Creative Thinking: Music and the Intuitive Art of Scientific Imagination': https://www.psychologytoday.com/gb/blog/imagine/201003/einstein-creative-thinking-music-and-the-intuitive-art-scientific-imagination [Accessed 16 April 2021]

3. Medeiros, J. (2018) 'Eminem's Life Story: From Bullied Dropout to Hip Hop Knockout': https://www.goalcast.com/2018/01/24/eminems-life-story-bullied-dropout-hip-hop-knockout/ [Accessed 16 April 2021]

4. Biography.com Editors (2021) 'Lady Gaga': https://www.biography.com/musician/lady-gaga [Accessed 16 April 2021]

5. Oprah Winfrey Network (2016) 'The Epiphany That Gave Jennifer Aniston "Total Peace" | The Oprah Winfrey Show | OWN': https://www.youtube.com/watch?v=O3U5gNo1h3A [Accessed 16 April 2021]

6. Akhtar, A. and Ward, M. (2020) '25 people who became highly successful after age 40': https://www.businessinsider.com/24-people-who-became-highly-successful-after-age-40-2015-6?r=US&IR=T [Accessed 16 April 2021]

7. Allan, T.J. (2015) 'How Michael Jordan's Mindset Made Him A Great Competitor': https://www.usab.com/youth/news/2012/08/how-michael-jordans-mindset-made-him-great.aspx [Accessed 6 June 2021]

8. Emmons, R.A. and McCullough, M.E. (2003), 'Counting Blessings Versus Burdens: An Experimental Investigation of Gratitude and Subjective Well-Being in Daily Life', *Journal of Personality and Social Psychology*, 84 (2): 377–389. DOI: 10.1037//0022-3514.84.2.377

Acknowledgements

First of all, I need to thank the most important person in my life. I already mentioned him before the book even began, but no amount of words could ever be enough for how much this man has done for me: my amazing husband, Ally. Thank you for being my Instagram husband, fellow weirdo and biggest fan. Being able to do this life with you is pure bliss.

I also need to thank everyone in the Hay House team who made it possible for my dream to become a reality...

Emily Arbis, this book wouldn't exist without you! You were able to see the vision when it was just a proposal, and after many meetings, emails, calls and late nights, you helped me to craft it into the final book that it needed to be. From one Dorset girl to another, a big heartfelt thank you for all of your effort, expertise and understanding.

Then it was on to Susie Bertinshaw and Stephanie Farrow for the copyedit. Thank you to you both for your attention to detail and for polishing the manuscript down into a succinct, neat, 60,000-word package that was ready to be printed and bound. Your help dotting the i's and crossing the t's was invaluable.

Thank you to everyone else at Hay House who helped to make this book happen: Michelle Pilley for running such an incredible publishing house; Jo Burgess, Lizzi Marshall, Portia Chauhan and everyone else in the PR and marketing departments who got the book out into the world; and last but not least, Kam Bains for giving me the book cover of my dreams!

I also feel obliged to thank Louise Hay for creating a safe home for people to share their spiritual message, and for being a living example of what we can achieve by going against the grain and being different. I'm also thankful to your spirit for visiting me in a dream, which is a story I'll tell another time!

Thank you to all of my wonderful clients – past, present and future – for supporting me in my work and trusting me enough to invest in yourselves. Extra special thanks to those who gave their written permission for me to tell their story in this book: Kori Kaur (IG: Koribella545), Chantelle O'Connor (IG: Cosmic_Chantelle), Colleen Clare (IG: ColleenClareYoga) and Sarah James Carter (IG: SarahJamesCarter).

There is another special person who allowed me to use their story as a case study – my loyal, lifelong friend Becca Rogers. My life has been 10x better because of you being in it, and I'm so grateful that the Universe brought us together at such a young age. Without you, I probably would have had an economics-induced mental breakdown, might have never discovered how much I love California, and would have laughed a lot less. You're the best friend a girl could ask for!

Another friend I want to thank is my spiritual bestie Rachel Alyce, who was also mentioned in this book. I have so much to thank you for, including helping me to set up my podcast, being so generous with your guidance and encouragement, and the many, many hours of voice notes. I can't wait to see what we go on to create in this lifetime!

A big note of thanks to my mother. Thank you for giving me my love of words and my connection to spirit, both of which enabled this book to be born. You have shown me endless love and what it means to be an amazing mother who cherishes her children. Thanks also to Vince, for always encouraging me to have a winner's mindset.

Love and gratitude to everyone else in my family who has shaped my journey, and to all of my other friends. I can't name you all, but you know who you are.

Lastly, thanks to YOU the reader for picking up this book. I hope it changes your life in the most wonderful of ways – and please let me know if it does!

ABOUT THE AUTHOR

ASMc

Liz Roberta is an award-winning spiritual coach who helps entrepreneurs to set up and scale successful spiritual businesses. She started her brand on Instagram in 2018 and has grown it to the point where she coaches people all over the world to help them align their life with their true soul calling.

After doing thousands of card readings for clients, Liz noticed that intuition was the most powerful tool of all for guiding people to what they want. She was named the 'Emerging Voice' of 2020 by *Kindred Spirit* magazine and a large part of her work is helping people share their authentic voice through writing and speaking.

Liz is the host of The Spiritual Success Podcast with Liz Roberta and writes the Millennial Manifestor blog at www.LizRoberta.com. She has been featured by BuzzFeed, Yahoo, Influencive, Medium, Thrive Global and Disrupt, as well as writing for publications such as *Soul & Spirit, Meditation Mag, Kindred Spirit* and *Spirit & Destiny*.

Outside of work, her passions are great coffee, living on the coast and really early mornings.

f   **iamLizRoberta**

@iamLizRoberta

www.lizroberta.com

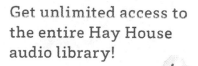

Hay House Podcasts
Bring Fresh, Free Inspiration Each Week!

Hay House proudly offers a selection of life-changing audio content via our most popular podcasts!

Hay House Meditations Podcast

Features your favorite Hay House authors guiding you through meditations designed to help you relax and rejuvenate. Take their words into your soul and cruise through the week!

Dr. Wayne W. Dyer Podcast

Discover the timeless wisdom of Dr. Wayne W. Dyer, world-renowned spiritual teacher and affectionately known as "the father of motivation." Each week brings some of the best selections from the 10-year span of Dr. Dyer's talk show on Hay House Radio.

Hay House Podcast

Enjoy a selection of insightful and inspiring lectures from Hay House Live events, listen to some of the best moments from previous Hay House Radio episodes, and tune in for exclusive interviews and behind-the-scenes audio segments featuring leading experts in the fields of alternative health, self-development, intuitive medicine, success, and more! Get motivated to live your best life possible by subscribing to the free Hay House Podcast.

Find Hay House podcasts on iTunes, or visit www.HayHouse.com/podcasts for more info.

HAY HOUSE
Look within

Join the conversation about latest products,
events, exclusive offers and more.

 Hay House

 @HayHouseUK

 @hayhouseuk

We'd love to hear from you!

Printed in the United States
by Baker & Taylor Publisher Services